LOVE OF LEARNING: DESIRE FOR JUSTICE

LOVE OF LEARNING: DESIRE FOR JUSTICE

Undergraduate Education and the Option for the Poor

Edited by
William Reiser, S.J.

Scranton: University of Scranton Press

Library of Congress
Catalog Card Number: 94-060876
ISBN 0-940866-41-2

University of Scranton Press
Chicago Distribution Center
11030 S. Langley
Chicago IL 60628

TABLE OF CONTENTS

LOVE OF LEARNING: DESIRE FOR JUSTICE

Introduction

Towards the end of the fall semester of 1992, a group of faculty members began speaking together about the meaning of the preferential option for the poor. The occasion of our coming together was our desire to contribute to the sesquicentennial events at Holy Cross College during the 1993-94 academic year. We decided to plan a symposium which would coincide with the anniversary of the deaths of the Jesuit educators at the Catholic University in El Salvador who were murdered on November 16, 1989. Because of its sudden and dramatic political repercussions, that event has been called the turning point in El Salvador's long, bloody civil war; it certainly has impressed upon Jesuits everywhere, and many of their colleagues, the risk of educating people for justice:

> But the turning point of the offensive, and of the war itself, came during the early hours of November 16th, when commandos scaled the back wall of the shady campus of the University of Central America, roused five Jesuit priests from sleep, ordered them to lie with their faces against the ground, and emptied automatic weapons into their brains. Before they departed, the soldiers killed a sixth priest, the Jesuits' cook, and her fifteen-year-old daughter. The scene they left behind -- the obliterated skulls of the priests, the green lawn soaked in blood and brains, the fantastically redundant number of spent cartridges -- was one of spectacular carnage.[1]

The phrase "option for the poor" originated within the Latin

---

1. Mark Danner, *The Massacre at El Mozote: A Parable of the Cold War* (New York: Vintage Books, 1994), 155-56.

American church. The idea figured prominently in the deliberations of the Latin American bishops assembled in the Mexican city of Puebla in 1979, although its roots went back to their meeting in Medellin, Colombia, eleven years earlier. The bishops at Puebla wrote: "With renewed hope in the vivifying power of the Spirit, we are going to take up once again the position of the Second General Conference of the Latin American episcopate in Medellin, which adopted a clear and prophetic option expressing preference for, and solidarity with the poor. . . . We affirm the need for conversion on the part of the whole Church to a preferential option for the poor, an option aimed at their integral liberation."[2]

But the option for the poor is relevant to the church in North America as well. The bishops of the United States adopted the following position in their strong (and celebrated) pastoral letter of November 1986 entitled *Economic Justice for All*. The bishops wrote:

> As individuals and as a nation, therefore, we are called to make a fundamental "option for the poor." The obligation to evaluate social and economic activity from the viewpoint of the poor and the powerless arises from the radical command to love one's neighbor as one's self. Those who are marginalized and whose rights are denied have privileged claims if society is to provide justice for all. . . . The "option for the poor" . . . states that the deprivation of the poor wounds the whole community. The extent of their suffering is a measure of how far we are from being a true community of persons. These wounds will be healed only by greater solidarity with the poor and among the poor themselves.[3]

The Society of Jesus would make this option its own in its Thirty-third General Congregation (1983), and the Society expected that every institution associated with the Jesuits would search for ways to review its mission in light of that option:

> The validity of our mission will also depend to a large extent on our

2. Quoted from par. 1134 of the final Puebla document. See John Eagleson and Philip Scharper, eds., *Puebla and Beyond* (Maryknoll, N.Y.:Orbis Books, 1979), 264.

3. See #87 and #88 of *Economic Justice for All: Pastoral Letter on Catholic Social Teaching and the U.S. Economy* (Washington, D.C.: United States Catholic Conference, 1986), 45, 46.

solidarity with the poor. For though obedience sends us, it is poverty that makes us believable. So, together with many other religious congregations, we wish to make our own the Church's preferential option for the poor. This option is a decision to love the poor preferentially because there is a desire to heal the whole human family.

The option for the poor is about a communion or solidarity which is "for the poor, with the poor, and against all forms of human poverty."[4]
The phrase "preferential option for the poor," together with its implications, is not merely pious rhetoric. It has been called "the most controversial religious term since the Reformers' cry, 'Salvation through faith alone'."[5] The deaths of the Jesuits in El Salvador brought home how perilous the notion of faith doing justice can be. Educational institutions are not only cradles of new ideas. They can also serve a prophetic role within societies as they bring critical, discerning attention to bear upon the fundamental problems of our time. Ignacio Ellacuria, one of the slain Jesuits and at that time Rector of the University, wrote:

[the University of Central America] often becomes an objective adversary to the economic, political, and military projects of the government. And it can be a powerful adversary, not because it has economic, political or military power, but because it has a social power based on the University word which is rational and Christian. And if this word is the word of truth, it becomes an uncomfortable power.[6]

The notions of justice and the option for the poor are linked. If it is true that faith and justice have become intrinsically connected in our contemporary understanding of what it means to be Christian, then the option for the poor may be what illumines the reason for that

4. From Decree 1, No. 48 of GC 33. See Donald R. Campion, S.J. and Albert C. Louapre, S.J., eds., *Documents of the Thirty-Third General Congregation of the Society of Jesus* (Saint Louis: The Institute of Jesuit Sources, 1984), 63.

5. See Donal Dorr, *Option for the Poor: A Hundred Years of Vatican Social Teaching* (Maryknoll, N.Y.: Orbis Books, 1983), 1.

6. *The Jesuit Assassinations* (Kansas City, MO: Sheed & Ward, 1990), 20.

connection. One writer has pointed out that "while the 'option for the poor' may be optional, acting justly is not."[7] Nevertheless, it is difficult to imagine a truly evangelical and truly virtuous approach to justice which does not issue from an option for the poor.

As faculty members from diverse disciplines we struggled together over the meaning of the preferential option for nearly a year. We believed that this was, and remains, something which needs to be talked about and understood. The urgency behind this option, which is nothing short of a conscious decision to insert one's mind and sensibilities, one's imagination and one's loyalties, into humanity's long struggle for a more just world, arises from our awareness of the enormous human misery caused by deep-seated injustice, which persists as strongly today as ever. None of us claims to have reached satisfactory answers to our collective and personal questions. How, we have asked ourselves, does the preferential option for the poor affect each of us in our respective disciplines? Is making this option a strictly private matter? Does it have any bearing on fields apart from religion and social ethics? Does language about the preferential option belong more properly in the chapel than in the classroom? And what is so threatening about this matter of preference for the poor that it would lead to murder? These are some of the questions and concerns behind the papers which are assembled here.[8]

THE SYMPOSIUM PRESENTATIONS

Following the delivery of each paper, there was lively discussion among both the panelists and the students and faculty in the audience. While the phrase "option for the poor" was first officially employed by the Latin American bishops, the whole church has now made that phrase its own. In his presentation, James Pratt (from the Department of Religious Studies) maintained that while many people in the church are *for* the poor, we have not yet achieved that solidarity with the poor

---

7. See Seamus Murphy, S.J., "The Many Ways of Justice" in the series *Studies in the Spirituality of Jesuits* 26:2 (March 1994), 27.

8. The Uruguayan theologian Juan Luis Segundo notes: "In any case, those who make an option for the poor are not the poor. This has been demonstrated over and over again. The option for the poor comes out of a middle class church that is aware of the suffering and oppression of the poor." See "Our Lady of Guadalupe: A Liberating Interpretation," *LADOC* (Latin American Documentation), 24 (Sept/Oct, 1993), 26.

which would help us to conceive and imagine a church *of* the poor.

Some wondered, however, about how exactly we go about becoming a church of the poor. Indeed, who are the poor? Do they comprise only the materially poor, or do they also include "the poor in spirit"? But if the category of the poor is broadened to include even people like us who might be spiritually but not materially poor, does that not rob the term "poor" of its critical meaning?

The theological justification of the option for the poor is based on a reading of the gospel story, and of the Old Testament, which sees Jesus firmly identified with the powerless and marginalized people of his time, even as the God of Israel had taken sides with the Hebrew slaves against their oppressors, and just as, centuries later, the God of the prophets had come to the defense of the poor, hungry and defenseless people of the land. But is this reading of Scripture excessively one-sided? And is it possible for us to make an option for the poor without actually standing alongside them in some concrete way?

Mary Morton (from the Department of Biology) went on to raise a number of far-reaching questions about how someone who teaches and does research in biology (or any other science) could incorporate the option for the poor into her work. Is there a way of teaching or communicating to students the profound human sensibility which underlies the choice to align oneself with the poor? Does the option for the poor ask us to change our classrooms and teach those whose slender means deprive them of the excellent educational facilities and opportunities we enjoy? Or does the option for the poor require that the very way we conceive the subject matter of our studies has to be transformed or "converted," as one member of the audience asked? Would it be fair to bring really poor students to our campus, given the probability that their educational backgrounds would be pretty weak? Is it fair not to? Is education capable of being an instrument of social justice? Would Holy Cross (or any other Jesuit college or university) be able to attract students if it became known as a "school for justice"? Would students be likely to enroll if we had a mandatory service program in all four years as part of the curriculum? If we can tolerate and defend other curricular requirements, why not a community service component?

In his paper, David O'Brien (History) suggested that many of the community service programs presently available to us can be conceived as expressions of an option for the poor. Through such programs, we stand to learn and to receive as much as we stand to teach and to give. In fact, the existence of service and outreach programs within an educational institution is itself a value statement. They reflect the curricular ideal of educating men and women for others.

David Gill (Classics) invited us to think about the apparent tension between the gospel injunction that we must love our enemies, and the gospel's clear opposition to every form of injustice. How are the poor, those who have suffered from political and economic oppression, to be expected to forgive their oppressors? Or is this expectation itself simply another way of oppressing them? Does it ask the poor, in the name of God, to swallow their anger and forget the causes of their misery? Or does the command to love one's enemy mean one thing when addressed to the poor and another thing when addressed to the rich? And are the rich being asked not to turn the poor into an enemy by resenting their aspirations for a fair share of this world's goods? Is the gospel's call to love of enemy, at least in the case of those of us who are so privileged, actually another way of translating the option for the poor?

Peter Perkins (Mathematics) demonstrated in a way both personal and moving how a college professor whose discipline has little to do with religious and ethical values can be called upon to wrestle with the option for the poor. What are we to do with our excess income? How might we set about replacing the widespread American dream of living affluently with the Christian desire (and mandate) to live simply? His paper was a sound reminder that the humanization and transformation of social structures and economic systems cannot occur, and would not prove lasting, unless those who are so materially and culturally advantaged are willing to change.

The next two presentations offered social and economic analyses, since without these we shall have only a vague understanding of who in our society really constitute the poor. Of all the people in our society, children are the more likely ones to be poor. While poverty among the elderly has tended to decline, poverty among children has been increasing. This has happened, David Hummon (from the Department of Sociology and Anthropology) pointed out, both because of changes in family structure and the growing feminization of poverty, where fathers fail to support their children. He called attention to the unequal distribution of wealth in our society; the top 20 percent of families control 80 percent of the nation's wealth. The paper by Charles Anderton and David Chu (Economics) points out the importance of examining public policy on the basis of its impact on the poor. Despite the good intentions of policy-makers, the poor will be most adversely affected by the negative impact of any public policy because they do not have the many resources possessed by the rich and the middle class. This paper further challenges us not to assume any facile solutions to the problem of poverty in American society.

The following three papers explore the demands which the option for the poor imposes upon us institutionally in terms of teaching, research, learning, and the College's presence within the local community. All of those who participated in preparing for the symposium were greatly affected and challenged by the truly seminal essay of Jon Sobrino, "The University's Christian Inspiration."[9] All of us realized, of course, that the situation of the Jesuit university in El Salvador is very different from our own; but at the same time we saw quite clearly that the option for the poor had to be an institutional option, and not just a personal option for individual faculty, students and staff. How do institutions change? Should we devise an "ethics across the curriculum" program which would render all of us, students and faculty alike, more sensitive to the awful human misery which exists in our world, and to our responsibility to do something about it? Would the poor include those who are financially well off but politically disenfranchised? How do we advocate the option for the poor within an educational institution without seeking to impose it? Can there be conversion toward the poor apart from being converted by the poor? Or, as Mauri Ditzler (from the Department of Chemistry) put it, has our educational system placed "the healthiest students in intensive care while it offers outpatient treatment to those with critical needs"?

Finally, Mary Ann Hinsdale (Religious Studies) looked at the relation between the option for the poor and women. Noting the vast numbers of poor women worldwide, she pointed out very clearly that the poor must be allowed to make their own option for whatever solutions will bring them out of their poverty. In many cases, the poor lack even the possibility of self-determination and self-expression. The bishops at Medellin viewed the poor as agents of their own empowerment. The rest of us must learn to struggle with them and on their behalf, which will frequently call for associating ourselves with women's aspirations for justice.

The aim of the symposium was to initiate a conversation about an extremely important topic. The papers were intended to be non-technical yet thought-provoking; we were college teachers trying to invite our students and our colleagues to join us in thinking about our

---

9. This can be found in Jon Sobrino, Ignacio Ellacuria, et. al., *Companions of Jesus: The Jesuit Martyrs of El Salvador* (Maryknoll, N.Y.: Orbis Books, 1990), 152-173.

responsibility to the world's poor and powerless. While our own discussions had been frank and animated, but for the most part inconclusive, audience response to the presentations was stimulating and encouraging. The option for the poor is not a topic with a limited shelf-life. It bears directly and seriously upon who we are as educators and learners, about how we conceive our mission and our responsibility to the truth.

The option for the poor even bears upon what constitutes real knowledge. It figures into how we read, study and discuss. It affects what we think and talk about. An option for the poor is going to influence not only what we study and what we choose to investigate, what material we teach and which courses students select; but because it is a choice, the option for the poor also confers upon knowledge a fundamentally moral character. The opportunity to learn creates a responsibility to learn wisely and to live compassionately.

It is no doubt true that making an option for the poor will call for different things from different people, depending upon the situation in which they find themselves. Yet, for reasons which should become clear in the course of these chapters, it is also true that an option for the poor will have a deep and lasting effect upon the way men and women come to understand themselves and the world. When the passion for teaching is informed by an option for the poor, our classrooms will become places where students encounter a constant mindfulness of their being connected to the poor and oppressed peoples of the world. And when the desire for learning is informed by an option for the poor, students will demand that their teachers be accountable to all those who hunger and thirst for justice.

The category of private property is out of place in the world of learning and ideas; it does not apply to knowledge and truth, or to the means of acquiring them. The words of the gospel are addressed to all of us:

> From everyone to whom much has been given, much will be required; and from the one to whom much has been entrusted, even more will be demanded. (Lk 12:48)

The possibility of knowing the truth gives rise to the moral responsibility of seeking the truth and living by it. The possibility of observing the world and understanding it creates the moral responsibility of looking carefully at its poverty and listening closely to its cries for bread, for justice and for respect. Otherwise we shall be like the gospel's rich man who in his feasting and merriment failed to notice the beggar starving at his gate. Opting for the poor means first noticing what is there to be seen outside our gate and then attempting to understand why what we have observed is there in the first place.

How can a theology call itself "Christian" if it bypasses the crucifixion of whole peoples and their need for resurrection, even though its books have been talking about crucifixion and resurrection for twenty centuries?

Let us hope that the day will come when oppression, demeaning and unjust poverty, cruel and massive repression cease to exist. On that day liberation theology will be obsolete, and this is the day that liberation theologians are working for, even though on that day they will be out of a job. But while oppression lasts . . . liberation theology is necessary and urgent. It is the only theology that defends the poor of this world -- or at least the only one that does so seriously. And let us remember that it is a theology that has martyrs like Ignatius of Antioch and Justin in the early centuries, which, as always, shows that at least it has been a Christian theology.

-- *Jon Sobrino, S.J.*

1.

A Church of the Poor and for the Poor

James F.X. Pratt, S.J.[10]

The past thirty years have been momentous ones for Catholic theology. The Second Vatican Council (1962-1965) was a watershed event; its importance cannot be emphasized enough. The face of Catholic theology has been permanently changed because of Vatican II. Since the council, such notions as "theology of liberation" and God's "preferential option for the poor" have become common parlance in our religious discourse. What do these terms mean? What impact do they have on believers today? Has the Catholic church suddenly developed a social conscience? What events made the church so aware of global poverty and structural injustice? What sort of concerns led Paul VI to call us to think in terms of the "complete development" of the whole human race "in the spirit of solidarity"?[11] Why has John Paul II insisted that the church must be aware of all those forces which oppose the world's becoming ever more human?[12]

---

10. James Pratt, S.J. teaches systematic theology at Holy Cross. He teaches courses on the problem of God and liberation theology, and is completing a doctoral dissertation on the theology of revelation.

11. See Pope Paul VI, *Populorum Progressio* (On The Development of Peoples), in Joseph Gremillion, *The Gospel of Peace and Justice: Catholic Social Teaching since Pope John* (Maryknoll, N.Y.: Orbis Books, 1976), 400.

12. John Paul II, *Redemptor Hominis* in *Proclaiming Justice and Peace: Documents*

13

Because the option for the poor has been so closely tied to the theology of liberation, let me first comment on what this theology is all about. The British theologian John McDade summarizes it this way:

> Liberation theology presents an understanding of Christian truth from the determinative experience of most human beings today: the experience of poverty and injustice. From this point of view, it presents the most sustained attempt by post-conciliar Catholicism to interpret Christian truth in solidarity with the "wretched of the earth" -- the weak and the hungry, the "non-persons" within social structures that exclude them and keep them in a powerless position. It is the most dramatic attempt by Catholic theology to locate the mystery of Christ within the *humanum*, within the complex of human experience and history: it affirms that only solidarity with the experience of humanity in experiencing and countering injustice and poverty provides the *locus theologicus* required by the character of the gospel. When confronted with the extent and depth of structural injustice in the world, Christian theology has the right to speak only if it is conducted in solidarity with those who are suffering, and is directed toward their liberation from oppression.[13]

The stress within liberation theology upon those at the bottom of society, and particularly with those who have been economically and politically oppressed, corresponds to a reading of the bible which finds the God of Israel firmly aligned with the voiceless and powerless ones of history. Methodologically, this calls for an adjustment in the way we think about major Christian beliefs. The experience of the poor becomes a privileged starting point for reflecting about God, Jesus, the church, sin and grace, sacraments, redemption, and so forth. Anyone wishing to explore this biblical foundation further should consult John Donahue's bibliographical essay "What Does the Lord Require?".[14]

---

from John XXIII - John Paul II, ed. Michael Walsh and Brian Davies (Mystic, CT: Twenty-Third Publications, 1985), 253.

13. John McDade, S.J., "Catholic Theology in the Post-conciliar Period," in Adrian Hastings, ed., *Modern Catholicism: Vatican II and After* (New York: Oxford University Press, 1991), 435.

14. See John R. Donahue, S.J., "What Does the Lord Require?: A Bibliographical Essay on the Bible and Social Justice" in the series *Studies in the Spirituality of Jesuits* 25:2 (March 1993).

This paper will examine three different understandings of the church. But since our understanding of the church is based on an understanding of the role of Jesus Christ, each section will first examine a picture of Jesus and then look at the ramifications this has for an understanding of the church today.

1. THE CHURCH

Many devout people understand Jesus to be the Son of God who came down to earth in order to free humankind from sin. Saint Ignatius of Loyola (1491-1556), the founder of the Society of Jesus, instructs those making the Spiritual Exercises to imagine this scene:

> The Three divine Persons, seated, so to speak, on the royal throne of their Divine Majesty. They are gazing on the whole face and circuit of the earth; and they see all the people in such great blindness, and how they are dying and going down to hell. . . . listen to what the persons on the earth are saying; that is, how they speak with one another, swear and blaspheme . . . Likewise, I will hear what the divine Persons are saying, that is, "Let us work the redemption of the human race." . . . I will consider what the people on the face of the earth are doing: How they wound, kill, go to hell, and so on. Similarly, what the Divine Persons are doing, that is, bring about the most holy Incarnation.[15]

In the Incarnation, the Second Person of the Trinity becomes human so that the redemption of humankind can occur. In Christ the divine and the human are united in a way never before imagined. Theologians today call this understanding of Jesus a christology "from above." Christology from above begins with the church's doctrinal understanding of Jesus as divine.

The Gospel of John is the chief biblical text which underpins a christology from above. In John's Gospel, with its exalted opening message "In the beginning was the Word, and the Word was with God, and the Word was God" (Jn 1:1), Jesus is portrayed as a divine figure who comes upon the human stage to deliver humankind from sin into the eternal life that God offers all of Jesus' followers. Christology from

---

15. *Ignatius of Loyola: The Spiritual Exercises and Selected Works*, ed. George Ganss, S.J. (Mahwah, N.J.: Paulist Press, 1991), 149.

above makes three claims. It claims (1) that the starting point for reflecting upon Jesus is the Christ of faith; (2) that through Jesus Christ God appears in human history; and (3) that the mission of Jesus basically was to redeem humankind from their sins. In a christology from above, the creeds from the early church councils at Nicaea (325), Constantinople (381) and Chalcedon (451) provide the theological basis for replying to the question "Who do you say that I am?" (Mk 8:29) with their clear affirmations that Jesus is truly God and truly human. Christology from above begins with dogmatic truths and then attempts to read these truths out of Scripture.

This portrayal of Jesus "from above" is conceptually neat and religiously appealing. It appears to undergird the liturgical experience of many Christian communities. Jesus is presented as a miracle worker who came to free humans from their sins. The "proof" of Jesus' divinity is his working miracles, and the greatest of all the miracles was his resurrection from the dead.

Corresponding to this christology there is also a church "from above." According to this view, the church was established by Jesus to continue his mission of redeeming humankind from sin. The salvation of souls becomes all important in the mission of the church. Jesus is presented as having explicitly handed down a blueprint for the church, which he personally established as the historical institution to continue his redemptive mission. The church becomes the place where people's sins can be forgiven. The church gives people the means to set themselves right with God. The seven sacraments become instruments for one's eternal salvation. The eucharist is seen as a sharing of the divine life as an indication of our restored relationship with God. Religion is a highly individualistic and private reality. But one major problem with this approach is that because the task of the church has been conceived as the salvation of one's own soul, religion becomes isolated from the other realities in our lives and piety tends to become a private, individualistic matter.

2. THE CHURCH FOR THE POOR

In light of the renewal of Catholic biblical scholarship and the Second Vatican Council, our understanding of Jesus and the church underwent a drastic change. Jesus was no longer pictured "from above"; thinking about Jesus began "from below." The methodology of christology from below proceeds along the following lines. First, the starting point for our reflection has to be the Jesus of history. Information concerning this historical person is to be found in the writings of the New Testament rather than in the traditional creeds. Second, the life of Jesus of Nazareth should be examined and interpreted in terms of social, historical, cultural and political categories, that is, through the social sciences, and not through traditional doctrinal categories. Third, the hallmark of Jesus' preaching and action was his commitment to the kingdom of God, and thus it is important to understand what the kingdom of God meant for him. All of Jesus' parables, miracles and actions explicate the meaning of the kingdom of God. Fourth, the primary approach to studying and interpreting the gospel texts is the historical-critical method.

In order to develop a christology from below, with its emphasis upon Jesus' humanness and its attention to experience (namely, Jesus' experience, the experience of the early Christian communities and our own experience today), and in order to understand the ministry of Jesus one must begin with the synoptic gospels, that is, the gospels of Mark, Matthew and Luke. However, one cannot fully appreciate these gospels without taking into account that there are various layers to their composition, and that these accounts have been composed in the light of Easter faith. Some of the events recorded by the evangelists may not be actual historical occurrences, but faith constructions of the evangelists (or of the early Christian communities) which have been retrojected into the life of Jesus. For example, the three passion predictions are most likely created by an evangelist; they do not originate with Jesus. So also the scenes of Jesus' temptation in the wilderness which we find in Matthew and Luke.

Theologians who advocate what is called the historical-critical method maintain that the synoptics contain a great deal of reliable historical material concerning Jesus of Nazareth. Jesus was a Jew of Palestine who proclaimed the kingdom of God. This proclamation triggered in the people a high regard for Jesus. Jesus was considered a person with authority -- which the political-religious leaders of the day regarded as a direct assault upon their power. Jesus undermined the foundations of the power structure of his day, a structure which excluded most of the people. The masses thus remained poor, marginalized and exploited.

The Jewish authorities so feared Jesus' power that they arranged to have him condemned to death. The parables, miracles and actions of Jesus held enormous political (as well as religious) dimensions. Jesus' primary enemy was not the Roman authorities but the Jewish leadership, who were the power-brokers both religiously and politically. The actions and words of Jesus resulted in his being tried as a political agitator. The religious authorities did not want to change the power structure that Jesus attacked in the name of the poor and exploited people in Jewish society. In one's appraisal of Jesus of Nazareth, it is impossible to separate politics and religion. The ministry of Jesus demonstrates that religion must offer guidance to politics.

Vatican II had three major themes: openness to the world, unity among Christians and the church viewed as the church of the poor. Cardinal Lecaro, a participant and major interpreter of the council, said:

> If we treat the subject of winning the poor for the gospel as just another one of the many themes which must occupy the attention of the Council we shall not satisfy the most real and most profound exigencies of our day (including our great hope of furthering the unity of all Christendom) -- indeed, we shall make it impossible for us to do so. . . The church herself is in truth the theme of the Council [especially insofar as] she is above all "the church of the poor."[16]

The council gave the first official articulation of the church's self-recognition that it was indeed a world church, but it only created the *possibility* for the church of the West actually becoming or expressing itself as a world church.

The majority of bishops at the First Vatican Council (1869-70) were European. Only during Vatican II does one observe the emergence of a significantly non-European episcopate, and the non-European bishops present at the council exemplified the increasingly international character of the church. This "world episcopacy," with and under the pope, acted at that "world council" as the supreme teaching and decision-making authority in the church.

More importantly, in the documents of Vatican II the church demonstrated its growing self-awareness that it was indeed called to be a world church. The Constitution on the Sacred Liturgy anticipated the use of vernacular languages in liturgical worship and foreshadowed the decline of Latin. Adoption of the vernacular signalled a clear example of the emergence of a world church, since the word of God and the sacramental rites would be heard and expressed in the native languages of the people. Inculturation -- adaptation -- was to become a

---

16. Quoted in Paul Gauthier, *Christ, the Church and the Poor* (Westminster, MD: Newman Press, 1965), 153.

constitutive element of theological method. The Roman church's cultural and theological perspective may not yet be attuned to the situations of North and South America, Africa and Asia. But the church must recognize the very real and diverse social and cultural differences which exist throughout the world and take these into account, if it is not to betray the council's intent. Even more to the point, however, is that being a world church above all implies being a church for and of the poor, since the poor constitute the vast majority of the people in our world. If it means anything, therefore, the process of inculturation calls for an immersion into the world of the poor.

Thus one major aspect of social and cultural diversity today is the situation of the poor in large parts of the world. Admitting or acknowledging the existence of poverty and destitution, however, is not the same as allowing the experience of the poor themselves to contribute to the reshaping of theology.[17] Since the council, the church has become increasingly sensitive to the condition of the poor, and one place where a local church has attempted to become a church which is truly of and for the poor is Latin America. The fresh theological perspective which emerged from the experience of the Latin American church was liberation theology. Liberation theology focuses on the life and experience of the poor. The gospel, it maintains, is above all for those who are economically disadvantaged, politically oppressed and socially marginalized. Liberation theology calls into question the theological view which suggests that one should not worry about the suffering and misery of this world because, if one leads a faithful life, God will reward us in the next. Liberation theology advocates that the whole church make a preferential option for the poor, because the God of Jesus has taken the side of the poor and oppressed. But being a church *for the poor* is not the same thing as being a church *of the poor*.

3. THE CHURCH OF THE POOR

The demographics of the church might startle those who live in North America and Europe. Most Catholics live south of the equator and the vast majority of them are people of color. John Paul II said:

> Nevertheless, in the light of Christ's words, this poor South will judge the rich North. And the poor people and poor nations -- poor

---

17. See, for instance, Jon Sobrino, *The True Church and the Poor* (Maryknoll, N.Y.: Orbis Books, 1984), and Leonardo Boff, *When Theology Listens to the Poor* (San Francicso: Harper & Row, 1988).

in different ways, not only lacking food, but also deprived of freedom and other human rights -- will judge those people who take those goods away from them, amassing to themselves the imperialistic monopoly of economic and political supremacy at the expense of others.[18]

With the renewed interest on Jesus in light of christology from below there has occurred a new understanding of Jesus as an advocate for the poor because Jesus himself was poor. He came from the backwaters: "Can anything good come from Nazareth?" (Jn 1:46) Jesus proclaimed the kingdom of God, God's preferential love for the poor: "Blessed are you poor, for yours is the kingdom of God" (Lk 6:20). Jesus was concerned with the poor, not out of a sense of philanthropy, but because he shared their condition. Jesus insisted that people could not love God and money (Mt 6:24). The secret of a Jesuit education is learning that one can never love both!

One can spiritualize the words of Jesus. When Jesus says, "Blessed are you poor, for yours is the kingdom of heaven" and "Woe to you that are rich, for you have received your consolation" (Lk 6:20,24), he intends that his words be taken at face value. Is it any wonder that all four gospels tell of Jesus being angry and resorting to physical violence in reaction to the defaming of the temple by money lenders?

What is the "mammon" that Jesus advised his followers not to serve? It is clearly more than money. Mammon is an emotionally loaded word. Perhaps we can describe mammon as that subtle desire to acquire many more things than we shall ever need. Mammon is what I do to money and what money does to me; we might call it "consumerism." Security and success, power and prestige, the possessions which make me appear privileged: all these are part of mammon.

If we are to approach Jesus from below, then it follows that we must understand the church from below, too. That is, the church's primary role is not going to be defined as saving "souls" but saving the poor. The root meaning of the word "salvation" means health. Instead of viewing the church as dispenser of the sacraments, we must learn to regard the church as called to speak on behalf of those who have no

---

18. Pope John Paul II, Homily at Edmonton Airport (Canada), September 17, 1984. See *Origins*, Vol. 14, No. 16 (October 4, 1984), 247.

voice, as John Paul II has done. The church is not for churchgoers; it is for the poor. In one sense, the church *is* the poor, because their life and their experience have been enshrined in the gospel story and are continually recalled whenever the community remembers the situation surrounding the suffering and death of Jesus.

The church of the poor is based on the primacy of the human, historical Jesus and the church which is called to continue his mission. The old formula "where the church is, there is Christ" (*ubi ecclesia, ibi Christus*) has to be reversed: where Christ is, there is the church, his people. The ecclesial Christ, that is, the Christ of the church's faith, represents flesh and blood human beings crying out for justice. The church becomes the agent of transformation for suffering men and women by continuing Jesus' proclamation of the reign of God. The humanity of Christ suffers in the poverty and deprivation of human beings, his sisters and brothers.

The poor of the world will challenge the church as it enters a new millennium. The church truly belongs to them, and they to us. As Christians living in the first-world, perhaps we shall eventually realize that it is not enough to be for the poor. In our affection and loyalty, in our decisions and actions, in our thinking and living we need to become ever more joined to them.

The theology of liberation seeks to understand faith from within this historical praxis . . . this is the fundamental hermeneutical circle: from humanity to God and from God to humanity, from history to faith and from faith to history, from the love of the Father to love of one's brothers and sisters, from human justice to God's holiness and from God's holiness to human justice.

-- From Gustavo Gutierrez,
   The Power of the Poor in History

2.

An Invitation to Conversation about Undergraduate Education and the Option for the Poor

Mary E. Morton[19]

I have entitled this paper "An *Invitation* to Conversation" for a number of reasons. I want to invite our students to be challenged by the issues we raise and to realize that many of their teachers also struggle with this topic. I would like invite our colleagues either to join in and to continue the discussions which have brought us together over the past year. The invitation is for an ongoing conversation, and I look forward to hearing your ideas and opinions, to know your concerns and questions. I hope that the conversation which we are starting today will lead to actions which will be consistent with our values. I have always viewed teaching as a conversation, both inside and outside of the classroom. I invite you to join in.

For the purposes of this paper, I prefer to focus on the poor as people who are educationally disadvantaged. There are doubtlessly

---

19. Mary E. Morton is a molecular neurobiolgist at Holy Cross. She received her Ph.D. in biochemistry from Dartmouth Medical School and was an N.I.H. postdoctoral fellow at University of Washington. Dr. Morton teaches courses for both biology majors and non-science majors. She and her undergraduate research students are currently investigating the developmental expression and regulation of signal transduction proteins in nerve and muscle.

other aspects of poverty which can and should also be explored. These factors would include, for instance, race, gender, ethnic background and socioeconomic status. Nevertheless, looking at the human condition worldwide, those who are oppressed, impoverished, and/or discriminated against for social, economic, ethnic, political or religious reasons are usually also those who have been deprived of educational opportunities. Although I am focusing on the poor in terms of their being educationally disadvantaged, I believe it is important to distinguish between *knowledge* based on experience (which the poor often have) and *education* based on formal, institutional schooling. While some might argue that a college education today may be more of a luxury than a necessity, I believe that an undergraduate education actually increases the options for the poor. I would like to initiate this discussion on the basis of some of my own personal goals, experiences and conflicts.

1. WHOM THEN SHALL I TEACH?

If I restate our topic of conversation as "Undergraduate education: options for the poor", there are three main questions to be discussed. All three of them are legitimate and important:

1. What options do the poor have to obtain an undergraduate education?

2. What can an undergraduate education provide to increase the options available to the poor?

3. What can an undergraduate education provide for the "elite" to increase the options available to the poor?

Let me proceed to the first question. What are the options which the poor have for obtaining an undergraduate education?

If we define "poor" as "educationally disadvantaged," the options available for these individuals are limited. Most colleges and universities require minimum grade and standardized test performance in order to be considered for admission. Although there is a growing awareness and concern that monetarily poor communities are also educationally poor, it is difficult to predict how many students from these communities would have fared well if properly nurtured in a different school system, or, in some cases, any school system. Add on factors such as malnutrition, improper health care, domestic violence, drug addiction and alcoholism, street violence, and/or civil war, and it becomes clear that an undergraduate education is *not* an option for the majority of teenagers in the world.

Even if a student does well in high school and wants to go to college, what are the options? With an educationally and monetarily disadvantaged background, the options are fairly limited. Tuition alone at a quality private school is prohibitively expensive, even for many middle-income families. Yet even given a free-ride scholarship, is it fair to place an impoverished, inner city student into the middle of a school like ours? Or a low income midwesterner into the middle of New England? The comparison is valid; even in the United States the cultural differences between neighborhoods, states, and regions can be vast. Different values and customs on even a small scale can be intimidating for an individual.

In addition to the cultural differences, however, there is the underlying problem of inadequate educational opportunities. Any individual who has not had modern biology in high school is going to struggle with the biology curriculum at Holy Cross. Even students who have done well in high school sometimes struggle with the courses at Holy Cross -- students who are from good schools in Massachusetts who are neither economically nor educationally disadvantaged. Is it fair to invite a student who does not have the course background to attend Holy Cross? Or should we offer to sponsor these students at a community college for two years and then have them join us on the hill? Or should we work as a nation to improve the K-through-12 school system throughout the country so that a majority of American children, from all socioeconomic backgrounds, have the same advantages and opportunities most of us have had?

Our second question: What can an undergraduate education provide to increase the options available to the poor?

No matter where a student chooses to attend college, one of the traditionally well-touted benefits of an education is increased marketability -- the ability to get a job or to obtain a better job with a greater likelihood of advancement and promotion. An education decreases the likelihood that an individual will remain a migrant worker, a farm hand, an unwed mother on welfare, or someone forced to survive earning only the minimum wage.

Although in the 1990's there have been fewer guarantees for employment, an undergraduate education increases the awareness of opportunities available to move up the economic ladder. Clearly, an individual who successfully obtains a college degree will no longer be educationally disadvantaged, and will be less likely to be economically disadvantaged.

And our third question: What can an undergraduate education provide to the "privileged" to increase the options available to the poor?

Unequal distribution of economic resources contributes to social inequality, something which is demonstrated very well in the papers by David Hummon and David Chu. I would argue that unequal distribution of educational resources further contributes significantly to this inequality. However, if the unequal economic distribution perpetuates this inequality, education provides a vehicle to redistribute the wealth -- informational and monetary. Therefore, it is important for all of us to learn about the disenfranchised and thereby heighten our awareness of their condition, if we are to contribute to the building of a new equilibrium.

One of the most attractive features about Holy Cross is the involvement of our students in the larger community. Through volunteer programs, such as serving meals at the Mustard Seed and tutoring high school students, or through consciousness-raising trips to Appalachia and Mexico, our students are learning about the social, political, economic, and educational inequalities in a small part of the world. Students return from these experiences realizing how much they take for granted and how privileged they are. However, they are also struck by the realization that the problem is not about the quality of people or quality of their values, but the quality and quantity of opportunities and options. We hope that by increasing awareness of these inequalities, our students will work to improve and increase the options available to the "poor."

However, it is important that education about others should not take place only in extracurricular ways. It is critical that education about the poor also take place in the classroom. Part of my responsibility as a professor is to teach and advise in a manner consistent with my values. For this reason I try to encourage students to think about others, not just about others conceived as those who are "not me," but about others as those who are "not *like* me."

2. WHERE THEN SHALL I TEACH?

Given the three questions I have just raised, I have to ask myself, "Is this institution the place for me?" Please do not get me wrong; I love what I do. But I wonder if I am really contributing to improve the world in any small yet meaningful way. Although some of my students have decided to become research biologists or neuroscientists, I am not convinced that they would not have chosen this option anyway.

I chose to teach at Holy Cross because of the excellence of the faculty and enthusiasm and interest of the students I met. In addition, the commitment of the students to service and volunteer efforts was appealing; the values of the students were consistent with my own. However, my sister, who teaches second grade in rural Indiana, works with impoverished youngsters from heartbreakingly unstable homes. She teaches them to read and write. She teaches them about self respect and self expression. The value in that is evident. I teach cellular and molecular neurobiology to students who are going to continue to do well for themselves. I do laboratory research that will never lead to a cure for cancer, AIDS, or even the common cold. Although "better living through chemistry" has been argued in the advertisement world, is "better living through cellular and molecular neurobiology" a reality? Can someone in the natural sciences discuss ethical dilemmas and challenges posed by recent scientific advancements? Is it my responsibility to do so?

I assume the responsibility at least to raise the ethical dilemmas and challenges in my field. I do not think that all faculty members at Holy Cross should be required to do so, but neither do I support the idea that ethics should be discussed only in courses which are entitled "Ethics" and offered through religious studies or philosophy departments. The advances made in molecular, medical, and cellular biology have contributed significantly to many of the ethical issues raised in this century. Therefore, it is important that those in the field also work to raise the level of public consciousness about those issues.

I admit freely to my students that I am not an ethicist. I have not been trained in the methodologies of this important field, and I am no more familiar with the jargon of ethicists than they are with mine. But even if I cannot supply any of the moral answers, I am at least aware of many of the questions which need to be considered.

3. HOW THEN SHALL I TEACH?

If I am committed to teach responsible science, how can I balance teaching fundamental biochemistry and discussing our responsibility to society? In a fact-based discipline, what are some of the approaches which can be used at least to encourage meaningful dialogue among our students?

Like most of my colleagues, I teach problem-solving skills. I try to provide my students with the resources and background to learn the "facts," the language of science. We then spend most of our time trying to apply those facts. In my upper division courses I inform students up front that it is assumed that they will have read the textbook prior to class, because most of our discussion is going to be based on the reading. This is not entirely the case, however. Most of

28 Option for the Poor

our discussions are actually based on what is *not* in the reading. We argue about assumptions which are made to be able to accept the unifying principles clearly stated in the books. We create ideas and hypotheses to explain observations. We invent experiments to test these ideas. In most cases, there are no "right" answers, although there are better answers. Because I teach biology, we discuss the underlying molecular and biochemical mechanisms behind Alzheimer's disease, Schizophrenia, Parkinson's Disease, Lou Gehrig's disease. Because I cannot teach biology in a vacuum, our discussions include a breakdown of the health care costs associated with neurological disease, the ethical dilemmas associated with genetic screening, and the social impact of an aging population.

In my non-majors course, we focus on the biology of disease causing critters -- viruses, bacteria, and protozoans, in addition to environmental and genetic diseases. My students are encouraged to write about the economic impact of the AIDS crisis, the ethics of vaccine trials in impoverished nations, or orphan drugs -- that is, drugs which are medically necessary but whose production is not profitable for the pharmaceutical companies. One semester a student stopped by my office after our class discussion about methods of developing a vaccine to prevent malaria. She was outraged that our government did not spend more money to help stop the ravages of this disease. The next week she stopped by again, furious that our government refused to develop drugs to fight sleeping sickness in Africa. A week later, billions more had to be spent on AIDS. Then Alzheimer's. By the end of our semester conversations, she realized that she had run out of money well before spring break.

There were two important lessons we both learned that semester. First, many of us skip the science sections and articles of newspapers and magazines, although our tax dollars support most biomedical research in this country. Therefore, many students are not aware of issues such as those I have raised, even at a superficial level. Second, money will not solve everything. A system of prioritization is needed and an ethical foundation needs to be built. We are trying to do this on a national level with the current attempts at Health Care reform. Imagine a global system! However, prioritization and ethical foundations need to be decided on the basis of knowledge within a discipline.

So, what does this have to do with our topic? How is teaching Neurobiology and Medical Detectives increasing the options for the poor?

Education not only provides an option for the "poor"; it also provides the means for the "elite" to contribute to changing the system in order to assist the poor, the elderly, the sick, the dying, and the socially oppressed. Although we do not have a cure for AIDS, we can teach students the scientific basis behind the search for a cure, the importance of learning the facts behind the "media hype", the effects of HIV infection on the poor and homeless, and the ethical questions associated with going to market with a drug before it has been tested. As informed citizens, they will be able to contribute to understanding the problems, educating the public, and working toward solutions.

Although we do not understand what causes Alzheimer's Disease, we do know how researchers are investigating the cause and I can teach why one approach may be better than another. I can tell you that more money is spent on convalescent care than research and I can tell you that this disease, like AIDS, impacts all of us. Although Alzheimer's Disease does not afflict only the uneducated, the uneducated are not in a position to contribute to alleviating the problem. It is important that our students realize where their tax money goes. I want to provide tomorrow's leaders with the foundation to be able to look up information and determine what is relevant. I do not want our graduates as doctors, lawyers, social workers, teachers, parents, economists, historians, artists, philosophers, or geniuses ever to say, "I did not know, did not know how to find out, and did not want to take the time to ask." I want to teach my students the problems, contributing factors, and methods of analyzing potential solutions. I want them to be concerned, devastated, heartbroken, shocked, and appalled. I want them to be moved to action that is founded on knowledge. This is our invitation.

The College of the Holy Cross is, by tradition and choice, a Jesuit liberal arts college serving the Catholic community, American society, and the wider world. To participate in the life of Holy Cross is to accept an invitation to join in dialogue about basic human questions: What is the moral character of learning and teaching? How do we find meaning in life and history? What are our obligations to one another? What is our special responsibility to the world's poor and powerless?

-- From the College Mission Statement

Our faith in Christ Jesus and our mission to proclaim the Gospel demand of us a commitment to promote justice and to enter into solidarity with the voiceless and powerless. This commitment will move us seriously to verse ourselves in the complex problems which they face in their lives, then to identify and assume our own responsibilities to society.

-- From Decree Four of the 32nd General Congregation of the Society of Jesus

3.
The Option for the Poor and Undergraduate Education

David J. O'Brien[20]

In this paper I would like to explore three areas: (1) the place of the option for the poor in recent Catholic thought, among Jesuits in particular; (2) some questions this option poses in an academic setting; and (3) some very tentative proposals about how to respond to all this at a liberal arts college like the College of the Holy Cross.

1. THE OPTION FOR THE POOR AND CONTEMPORARY CATHOLICISM

During and after World War II, many Catholics, like most decent people, felt compelled by the tragic events of the war and the slaughter of millions of Jews to examine their church and its place in modern history. Extreme nationalism and anti-Semitism had flourished in some Catholic areas, many Catholics had warmly supported fascist movements across Europe, and the church had cooperated with fascist states in Italy, Austria, Spain and Portugal. In addition, many

---

20. David O'Brien is Loyola Professor of Roman Catholic Studies at the College of the Holy Cross where he directs the Peace and Conflict Studies Program. An American historian, his most recent book is *From the Heart of the American Church: Catholic Higher Education and American Culture* (Orbis Books, 1994).

wondered whether the popular understanding that the church *alone* offered the means to salvation after death had encouraged a preoccupation with the welfare of the church, and a certain political and intellectual irresponsibility.

That rethinking burst into the open with the arrival of Pope John XXIII in 1958 and especially at the Second Vatican Council. In *Pacem in Terris* (1963), Pope John turned the church away from its long defensive preoccupation with itself and toward a pastoral concern for the wider human family. He affirmed human rights that Catholicism had long denied and asked Christians to think of Christ's church as humanity's partner and friend, sharing the universal responsibility to make peace by reforming human society on the basis of truth, justice, charity and freedom. The council endorsed this turn away from a triumphalist sense of the church as an exclusive channel of other worldly salvation to one which made its own "the joys and the hopes, the griefs and anxieties of the men and women of this age, especially those who are poor or in any way afflicted," to use the opening words of the council's Pastoral Constitution on the Church and the Modern World.

The beginning of renewal for Christians, then and now, was this new realism, this willingness to look around and see "the signs of the times" through the eyes of faith. When Pope John looked around, he saw people more conscious of their dignity, gifted with remarkable intelligence which gave them new technologies capable of bringing their world to self-destruction, but equally capable of bringing to fulfillment of the age old dream of a single human family. He hoped Christians could help nudge history along that better road. In Latin America, Catholic pastoral workers, inspired by the council, looked around and saw that their church devoted almost all its resources to a tiny group of well to do, respectable people, creating an island of faith amid a sea of human misery. So they decided, after prayerful deliberation, to make an "option" to serve the poor. In the United States, in those years following the council, people looked around and saw assassinations, racial conflict, urban riots, and a seemingly endless war in Vietnam. The bishops belatedly endorsed the struggle for civil rights, they launched the Campaign for Human Development in 1968 as their own "war on poverty," and, in 1971, they became the first bishops in modern history to oppose their own government's conduct of a war. At about the same time two Holy Cross students looked around, made their own option for the poor and began the Catholic Worker house, the Mustard Seed.

In their desire to provide needy people with food, clothing and shelter, at a personal sacrifice, those Holy Cross students were not alone. Father Pedro Arrupe, Superior General of the Society of Jesus, had been in Nagasaki when the second atomic bomb fell. Like Pope John, he was remarkably alert to the aspirations of the world's victims. In the wake of the Vatican Council, he suggested that his Jesuits, too, look around and rethink their mission. Jesuits are best known as educators, and Father Arrupe hoped they would continue to teach. "Our prime educational objective must be to form men (and women)-for-others," he said in 1973. He spelled out what that required:

> First, a firm determination to live more simply. . . Second, a firm determination to draw no power whatever from clearly unjust sources. . . Third and most difficult a firm resolve to be agents of change in society, not merely resisting unjust structures and arrangements, but actively undertaking to reform them.21

Sparked by his vision, his fellow Jesuits, gathered in General Congregation, made their own "preferential option for the poor" as the governing condition for all Jesuit ministry. For Jesuits, their work became "the service of faith, of which the promotion of justice is an absolute requirement." Since then, Jesuits around the world have struggled to renew their apostolates, and the institutions with which they are associated, in light of this commitment. In the United States, however, the twenty-eight colleges and universities sponsored by the Society of Jesus have had only limited success in integrating this vision into their fundamental work of research and teaching.

Pope John Paul II, always responsive to suffering, has had many things to say about the meaning of the phrase, "option for the poor," but he has made the option his own and a centerpiece of modern Catholic self-understanding. The idea is complicated. It as a theological statement, having to do with the witness and teaching of Jesus, and what he reveals about God and about humanity. For scholars it is also a hermeneutical principle, demanding that one self-consciously examine things from the point of view of the poor. And it is an ethical imperative, it makes demands, though it is far from clear exactly what those demands are. While learned theologians and prayerful Christians ponder such questions, there can be no doubt that there are substantial scriptural warrants, and compelling reasonable arguments, that making

21. Pedro Arrupe, S.J., *Men for Others* (Jesuit Conference: Washington, D.C., 1973), 15.

an option for the poor and translating that option into practice is what a
fully human life, and therefore a fully Christian life, is all about.

2. THE OPTION FOR THE POOR AND HIGHER EDUCATION

At every level the Catholic Church has become ever more insistent
that its educational mission cannot be confined to matters of personal
morality and eternal salvation, but must be tested by its contribution to
peace, justice and human liberation. John XXIII issued a powerful
appeal for a Christian education appropriate to the magnitude of the
church's mission in the modern world and the new potential of an
educated laity:

> Indeed, it happens in many quarters and too often that there is no
> proportion between scientific training and religious instruction: the
> former continues and is extended until it reaches higher degrees,
> while the latter remains at an elementary level. It is indispensable,
> therefore, that in the training of youth, education should be
> complete and without interruption; namely, that in the minds of the
> young, religious values should be cultivated and the moral
> conscience refined, in a manner to keep pace with the continuous
> and ever more abundant assimilation of scientific and technical
> knowledge. And it is indispensable too that they be instructed
> regarding the proper way to carry out their actual tasks.[22]

This plea is repeated again and again in the major documents of
the modern church, from Vatican II through the speeches and
encyclicals of John Paul II. The American bishops, for example,
argued in 1973 that:

> The success of the Church's educational mission will also be judged
> by how well it helps the Catholic community to see the dignity of
> human life with the vision of Jesus and involve itself in the search
> for solutions to the pressing problems of society. Christians are
> obliged to seek justice and peace in the world. Catholics
> individually and collectively should join wherever possible with all
> persons of good will in the effort to solve social problems in ways

---

22. Pope John XXIII, *Pacem in Terris*, in David J. O'Brien and Thomas A. Shannon,
eds., *Renewing the Earth: Catholic Documents on Peace, Justice and Liberation*
(Garden City, N.Y.: Doubelday & Co., 1977), 161.

which consistently reflect Gospel values.23

In their much discussed pastoral letters of the 1980's the U.S. bishops repeatedly called upon Catholic colleges and universities to incorporate peacemaking and justice seeking into their teaching and research. "Those who enjoy the benefits of Catholic higher education have the obligation to provide our society with leadership on matters of justice and human rights," the bishops wrote at one point.[24]

But education is done by educators, and in higher education the educators are learners themselves. There can be no education for justice and peace without scholars so committed. And church leaders have spoken to them as directly as possible. At Hiroshima in 1981, for example, John Paul II did not hesitate to tell a largely non-Christian audience of scholars and scientists that all of us together have to try to transform the social order and we will do it only if we recognize the imperatives of love:

> From now on, it is only through conscious choice and through a deliberate policy that humanity can survive. . . The task is enormous, some will call it a utopian one. . . The building of a more just humanity or of a more united international community is not just a dream or a vain ideal. It is a moral imperative, a sacred duty (requiring) a fresh mobilization of everybody's talents and energies. . . The construction of a new social order presupposes over and above the essential technological skills a lofty inspiration, a courageous motivation, belief in [humanity's] future, [human] dignity, [human] destiny. . . In a word, a [person] must be loved for his [and her] own sake.25

Professors, students and staff at colleges and universities from time to time try to do what the church has done, look around to see the world as it really is and ask, in light of what we believe, who we are

23. See *To Teach as Jesus Did* (1973) in *Pastoral Letters of the United States Catholic Bishops*, III (Washington, D.C., 1983), 308.

24. "Catholic Higher Education and the Pastoral Mission of the Church," in *Pastoral Letters*, IV, 410.

25. John Paul II, "Humanity Must Make a Moral About Face," *Boston Pilot*, March 6, 1981.

and what are we doing. We think, for example, of the holocaust. Standing at Auschwitz, experiencing its brutal reality, people ask: what is the meaning of this place for me, as a person, as a student, as a professor? Or stand, as a friend of mine once did, with Mother Theresa in Calcutta, and ask how one can affirm the presence of a loving God, or even affirm the reasonableness of life, as professors must, in the midst of so much suffering. Jesuits at the University of Central America in El Salvador looked around at their nation's violent struggle, and renewed their teaching and research as service to the poor; six of them, along with two women co-workers, were killed because they were considered subversive. Students from Holy Cross occasionally visit with poor people in Worcester, or in Appalachia, or in Mexico. In the midst of that experience, many ask themselves what it means to be the persons they are: mainly persons of Christian faith, wishing to affirm a relationship of friendship, perhaps solidarity, with those people, the poor. Some emerge from that reflection thinking differently about their education and their lives.

There are many debates about what to do about this option for the poor, but notice that it begins with looking around, as realistically as possible, and thinking about ourselves and what we believe in light of that experience. The option for the poor is a matter of our looking hard at "them," the poor, but also of their looking hard at us, and our willingness to see ourselves through their eyes. Then come the questions, and the challenges.

In 1978, Holy Cross awarded an honorary degree to Cesar Jerez Garcia, S.J., at that time provincial of the Jesuits in Central America. Jerez Garcia, a Chicago-trained social scientist, and his fellow Jesuits in Guatemala had been threatened with death if they did not leave that country. The honorary degree was a small sign of support. Canisius College in Buffalo invited Jerez Garcia to deliver the commencement address a few days after the Holy Cross graduation. There he told the assembled graduates, their teachers and families, that he wondered whether Jesuit education was helping to ease their path into what he obviously regarded as a unjust and repressive economic system, or whether they had been awakened by their education to a sense of social obligation that would influence not only their political behavior but their vocation. He became very concrete, saying he hoped they would not go to work for any of a list of multinational corporations he named:

> Do you plan to use your degree for your own profit, be it profit in the form of money or power status or respect? Will you end up with General Motors or Morgan Trust, with Chase Manhattan or Abbot Laboratories, with Goodyear or Boeing. . . Will you become

people who use your knowledge for the furtherance of justice . . . or live the good life of manipulated, unconcerned people in suburbia who grant honorary degrees to people from the Third World but refuse to join them in the fight for justice and liberty for the poor of the world?[26]

This was a strong message, familiar to most Jesuits and to people informed about contemporary Catholic life, but undoubtedly shocking to the graduates and their families. That surprise, tinged by anger, would have been felt at Notre Dame or Holy Cross or any Catholic college. It constituted, and still constitutes, a serious indictment of Catholic higher education.

3. THE OPTION FOR THE POOR AT HOLY CROSS

Yet, Holy Cross has hardly ignored the option for the poor. In the spring of 1970, at the request of the graduating class, retiring Holy Cross President Father Raymond Swords delivered the commencement address. It was a special time, the end of a year marked by student strikes in December and May. Here is part of what Father Swords said:

> [W]hat you are commencing here is -- I believe and hope -- something new in the history of Holy Cross . . . the beginning of a lifelong commitment to fundamental change -- social and poltical and cultural and religious. . . [T]he catalytic events of the past six weeks -- Cambodia, Kent State, Augusta and Jackson -- and their reverberations on this hill, have revealed the depth of your feeling . . . You have made your stand, openly and publicly, for all to see. It is a stand for life, for peace, for justice for *all* -- American and Asian, black and white, rich and poor, young and old. . . There can be, and there will be, debate over the best means of achieving these goals. . . But the goals themselves are non-negotiable. And, at the most fundamental level, they are inseparable because they flow from a common source, a radical understanding of [humanity] that is as old as the Bible and as new as the Berrigans.[27]

---

26. Cesar Jerez Garcia, S.J., Commencement Address (typescript in author's possession).

27. Raymond J. Swords, S.J. in *The Holy Cross Quarterly* (Spring 1970), 40-48.

Perhaps when the class of 1970 returns for its twenty-fifth reunion, its members will compare notes about that pledge. As for the College, Father John Brooks has regularly renewed its commitment to educate "men and women for others." Individual professors, members of the staff and many, many students make innumerable personal efforts to act on this vision. Faith and justice and the option for the poor mark all the work of our remarkable campus ministry program. Recently the Worcester and Boston alumni began sponsoring a student to work with the poor during the summer. Swords' pledge, in softer language, is renewed on ceremonial occasions, as it was when the El Salvador Jesuits were killed. This symposium constitutes another of those moments of rededication.

But it would probably be fair to say that neither the church, nor its colleges and universities, nor the American Jesuits, nor we at Holy Cross are satisfied that we have properly understood and acted upon the option for the poor. There is good work being done, of course. Among the models are the PULSE program at our sister school, Boston College, through which students fulfill a philosophy requirement by combining service to the poor with examination of basic texts in philosophy; Notre Dame's Center of Social Concern, located in a building near the library entrance, offering an array of service-learning opportunities, among them an intense urban plunge during Easter vacation and Andrews Fellowships, stipends for summer service through Notre Dame alumni clubs; major new urban initiatives at Fordham, Marquette and Santa Clara, joining university and neighborhood resources in programs of housing, economic development, education and crime control; or an innovative initiative at Loyola of Chicago to link university research with area community organizations. The list is a long one, for Catholic and for non-Catholic colleges and universities.

But haunting questions remain, even within the most creative programs and among the most compassionate people. And no one has a blueprint for education for faith and justice, or for research and teaching appropriate within an option for the poor. There is plenty of room for experimentation. Let me suggest three possible projects, chosen partly on the basis of low cost, at a time when budgets allow little room for new programs.

First, Social Concerns Day. Several years ago we initiated a social concerns week, which still takes place; but interest has waned. Perhaps we could renew our commitment, now focused on a single day each year (or each semester) when all of us would take time to explore the option for the poor in the specific setting of our work together. Perhaps a film or lecture the night before would focus the discussion. Professors would take up the topic in their classes, combining classes in some cases, inviting speakers where appropriate, all centering the question on their discipline, on the work of teaching and research we do together. Other offices of the College might hold their own staff days or open houses to discuss the challenge as it relates to their work. It would be an annual occasion to implement one small piece of our mission statement, the invitation to conversation around central human questions of meaning and social responsibility, in this case focused on the question of our obligation to the poor and powerless.

Second, Community Service. This is one of today's major subjects in higher education, providing a remarkable opportunity to open dialogue about the meaning of higher education in a world scarred by massive poverty. Community service is an area in which Holy Cross already has a remarkable record. Could we not come up with some creative projects to integrate service into our curriculum through expanded internship opportunities, departmental practicums where appropriate, better training and support for student leaders in community service, faculty association with the Mexico and Appalachian programs? Could we not design pre-social service and pre-public service programs comparable to pre-law and pre-med, and use our present concentrations to expand opportunities for our students and faculty to think through the relationship between research, learning and social responsibility? To begin, it might be well to organize a retreat for faculty, staff and student leaders most deeply engaged with community service. In addition, it might be well to resurrect a proposal made last year to the Board of Trustees for an office of community relations to explore ways in which the College can relate more creatively to the local community.

Third, Capstone Courses. Most of all, the option for the poor is something to be incorporated into our lives. Seeing the world and ourselves through the eyes of the poor, we are asked to think in new ways about our work, our politics, our relationships to one another. For undergraduate education, the horizon is beyond the campus. The learning is tested in the way we live as citizens and, for Christians, as disciples. We faculty have been trained in disciplines whose best practitioners often seem to believe their work has nothing to do with such matters. But of course it does, even in the most scientific of sciences, as we learn every time there is a war.

Capstone courses might center on vocation, asking how

knowledge is used in our society, how careers and vocations are structured in institutions, how persons can in concrete terms use their skills and talents "for others" or for a common good which includes everyone. Such courses, making the much promised integration of liberal arts education real, might provide a fitting conclusion to the undergraduate experience. Experimenting with such courses, perhaps beginning in the concentrations and in the divisions (humanities, sciences and social sciences), might open up better ideas for creative reform of the curriculum.

Perhaps this sounds a bit too Catholic for a community increasingly marked by, and valuing, diversity. Yet the heritage and responsibility of Holy Cross as Catholic intersects with the requirements of higher learning at a time of considerable confusion. In its earliest stages, Catholic higher education in the United States was designed to help Catholics survive, in part by recruiting and training priests and sisters. In its second stage, picking up speed after World War II, Catholic colleges and universities helped Catholics move up the social and economic ladder, helped the children of immigrant outsiders become authentic insiders. In the first stage people like the Jesuits struggled to create colleges and universities. Later they worked hard to make them very good colleges and universities. The model for the first stage was the priest helping his people build a church and root themselves in America and its local communities. During the second stage there were some new models: the talented, tough, ambitious veterans of World War II and their sisters becoming doctors and lawyers and businessmen and women, carving out for themselves and their people a place at the center of American life: Democrat Bruce Babbitt and Republican John Sears, my classmates at Notre Dame; Abigail McCarthy from St. Catherine's and her husband Eugene from St. John's; Mary McGrory from Emmanuel; Edward Bennett Williams, a symbol for Holy Cross.

Today, in our work together at Holy Cross, a more diverse community is defining a third stage. And who will be the models of the next generation? People, perhaps a shade less Catholic, finding the boundaries of churches and nations more blurred, ready to ask some tough new questions about religion and church, patriotism and politics, people ready to build communities which are communities of conscience and families which are authentic partnerships. They are out there already: A nurse building a Catholic Worker hospice for terminally ill AIDS patients in Oakland. A doctor with the World Health Organization in east Africa. In Baltimore, a community organizer developing affordable housing and another creating a new way to support high school students through the perils of urban poverty and violence. A graduate student studying ethics and arms control in hopes of improving the quality of public discourse, then working awhile in social services until his wife gets her law degree. A young woman serving as social action director for a Jesuit province. Another young couple with several children who decides that she will work at a job she loves while he works at home with the children, and provides leadership in ministry and religious education in their parish. A Catholic Worker couple facing jail for challenging the Trident submarine and building a "family for others" in the inner city. A Hartford insurance executive helping other lay Catholics discover opportunities to make the search for human dignity part of their everyday experience at work.

The option for the poor at a college like ours, then, has to do with forming a working community where people, young and not so young, can form convictions, become confident about compassion, sharpen their wits, turn talent and knowledge to use for the world, and perhaps find some friends for their journey. If we could do that even a little bit, we would make a significant contribution to our society, and to American higher education.

There is a story that one day in Auschwitz, a group of Jews put God on trial. They charged him with cruelty and betrayal. Like Job, they found no consolation in the usual answers to the problem of evil and suffering in the midst of this current obscenity. They could find no excuse for God, no extenuating circumstances, so they found him guilty and, presumably, worthy of death. The Rabbi pronounced the verdict. Then he looked up and said that the trial was over: it was time for the evening prayer.

-- Karen Armstrong
A History of God

4.
"Love Your Enemies" and the Option for the Poor

David Gill, S.J.[28]

Jesus was himself poor and he spoke to poor and oppressed people in their real lives. He did not talk much about economics or politics, although he was clearly suspicious of both wealth and power. His immediate message was about the imminent coming of the Kingdom of God and how his followers should live in order to make themselves ready for it. This Kingdom, he claimed, was to have a special place in it for the poor, the afflicted, the meek, the hungry, the merciful, the pure in heart, the peacemakers and the persecuted. To these people he said that they should love their enemies and not seek vengeance against them. The New Testament writers took these commands seriously and passed them on and adapted them for their readers, the first two generations of the followers of Jesus.

Almost every aspect of this teaching of Jesus has been -- and continues to be -- matter for dispute. Did he actually even say these things? And if he did, whom did he mean by "enemies"? What could loving them involve? And what did he and his first followers think would be achieved, if anything, by doing so? How could Jesus in

---

28. At the time of the seminar, David Gill, S.J. was Rector of the Jesuit Community at Holy Cross and teaching in the Classics Department. He is currently Associate Professor of Classics at Boston College. He is a member of Pax Christi and of the Agape non-violent community in Hardwick, Massachusetts.

justice have told poor and oppressed people not to resist their oppressors? And what relevance do these commands have for Christians and others today, for whom the Kingdom has obviously not come and who, both rich and poor, live in vastly different social and economic conditions from the original hearers of the message?

The relevant texts are the words of Jesus as reported by the evangelists Matthew (5:38-48) and Luke (6:27-36) and some of the parallels in the New Testament. As will become evident, my paper owes a great deal to Willard M. Swartley's excellent recent collection of essays, *The Love of Enemies and Nonretaliation in the New Testament*.[29]

JESUS' TEACHING ON LOVE OF ENEMIES

The gospel texts share several elements and apparently rely on a common source, an earlier collection of the sayings of Jesus. Most scholars agree that the love command and at least some of the illustrative material go back to Jesus himself. Each evangelist adapted the source to his own audience and circumstances, but both convey essentially the same message. Enemy love is an absolute command of Jesus. It is a positive attitude which includes praying for the adversary. It does not seem to be based on any hope of return from the enemy. God will reward it, but the primary motive is imitation of the Heavenly Father, who also loves his enemies, and whose sons and daughters the disciples of Jesus are.[30] The examples also reveal something of the social-economic context of their audience: poverty leading as a matter of course to forced labor, begging, borrowing, stealing, spiteful behavior and (possibly) violence. The question is how enemy love

---

29. Louisville, KY: Westminster/John Knox, 1992. Reviewed by me in a forthcoming issue of *Horizons*. The aim of the collection is to combine critical exegesis with serious moral and theological reflection on Christian responses to questions of nonviolence and peacemaking. I would also like to thank my colleagues in the Option for the Poor seminar at Holy Cross for criticisms and suggestions. Thanks also to Suzanne Shanley of the Agape Peace Community in Hardwick, MA, for help in focusing some of the issues regarding nonviolence, pacifism and giving unto Caesar.

30. For questions of the evangelists' sources (Q), their use of it in their own situations and their relation to one another, and for recent bibliography on the subject, see my essay "Socrates and Jesus on Nonretaliation and Love of Enemies," *Horizons* (1991): 246-252, and Swartley passim.

relates to this situation.

The gospel texts are given here, in parallel fashion, following Luke's order, which is generally thought to be closer to that of the common source from which both evangelists drew. Which evangelist actually comes closer to Jesus' own formulation in individual cases is disputed.

LUKE 6:27-36	MATTHEW 5:38-48

<table>
<tr><td></td><td>43You have heard that it was said,
"You shall love your neighbor
and hate your enemy."</td></tr>
<tr><td>27But I say to you that hear,
Love your enemies
do good to those who hate you,
28bless those who curse you,
pray for those who abuse you.</td><td>44But I say to you,
Love your enemies</td></tr>
<tr><td></td><td>and pray for those who persecute you.
38You have heard that it was said,
"An eye for an eye
and a tooth for a tooth."
39But I say to you,
Do not resist one who is evil.</td></tr>
<tr><td>29To him who strikes you on the cheek,
offer the other also;
and from him who takes away
your cloak
do not withhold your coat as well.</td><td>But if anyone strikes you on the right cheek
turn to him the other also;
40and if any one would sue you and take your cloak
let him have your cloak as well;
41and if anyone forces you to go one mile,
go with him two miles.</td></tr>
<tr><td>30Give to every one who begs from you;
and of him who takes away your goods, do not ask them again.
31And as you wish that men would do to you, do so to them.
32If you love those who love you, what credit is that to you?
For even the sinners love those who love them.
33And if you do good to those who</td><td>42Give to him who begs from you, and do not refuse him who would borrow from you.

[cf. Mt 7:12]

46For if you love those who love you what reward have you?
Do not even the tax collectors do the same?
47and if you salute only your</td></tr>
</table>

do good to you,
what credit is that to you?
For even sinners do the same.
³⁴And if you lend to those from
whom you hope to receive,
what credit is that to you?
Even sinners lend to sinners,
to receive as much again.
³⁵But love your enemies,
and do good, and lend,
expecting nothing in return;
and your reward will be great,
and you will be sons of
the Most High;
for he is kind to the ungrateful
and the selfish.

³⁶Be merciful,
even as your Father is merciful.

brethren,
what more are you doing than others?
Do not even the Gentiles do the same?

⁴⁵so that you may be sons of your
Father who is in heaven;
for he makes his sun rise on
the evil and on the good,
and sends rain on the just
and on the unjust.
⁴⁸You, therefore, must be perfect,
as your heavenly Father is perfect.

Matthew distinguishes between enemy love and nonretaliation against "the one who is evil." Though this gives a slightly different emphasis to some of the examples, the result is basically the same, since the evil person is presumably an enemy. Love, in the first instance, demands praying for him when he persecutes (Matthew) and abuses (Luke) you, and blessing and doing good to him when he curses and hates you (Luke).

The point of a slap in the face lies in the personal insult, presumably undeserved. The response is not only not to strike back but to offer the other cheek as well. What is supposed to happen next is left to our imagination.

In the example of the coat and the cloak, Matthew seems to imply the potentially hateful situation where the disciple owes or wants to borrow money and the other party demands his inner garment as payment or surety. Rather than go to litigation, Jesus says, simply give him your (more expensive) outer garment as well -- and presumably leave yourself naked. Luke's image is one of theft, in which someone "takes away" the (outer) cloak and the response is to let him take the (inner) coat as well, with the same result.

Only Matthew has the example of the "extra mile," which

probably refers to the well attested practice of forced labor in which a government official requires a person to work without pay in building or repairing a road or carrying a burden for a specified distance. As in the previous two examples, the response is a kind of doubling of the unjust or oppressive demand. Luke may have omitted it as less relevant to his audience, or Matthew may have added it. We cannot be certain.

Both versions recommend generosity to beggars, but where Matthew has lending "to him who would borrow from you," Luke again seems to imagine a situation of robbery or theft, in which the disciple is told not to seek to get back what was taken.

Next Luke (alone) quotes the Golden Rule (verse 31). At first this looks like a counsel of self-interest, but he quickly corrects that impression with what he places next. The material and the order is like Matthew's, but the variations seem designed to make the point that "doing unto others" is not a strategy of reciprocity. The first question, now in the context of the Golden Rule, apparently wants to reinterpret the rule as entailing an obligation to love the enemy first, even though one has not received any love in advance. The second seems to be aimed at the common Greek ethic of reciprocity: help your friends, hurt your enemies. Luke implies that even in its positive aspect of mutual benefits among friends the ethic is not enough for Christians. The third question sharpens the issue of money lending, over against Matthew, by explicitly excluding the motive of repayment.

Matthew and Luke agree on the motive for enemy love. It makes one a child of God, or rather indicates that one already is. The quality in God which grounds the imperative is God's perfection (Matthew) or mercy (Luke), as shown in the fact that God treats both enemies and friends in the same way, with sun and rain (Matthew) and with kindness (Luke).

Both Matthew the Jew and Luke the Gentile came from ethical traditions which divided the world into friends and enemies and recommended treating each accordingly. They and the Christian oral and written tradition behind them were convinced that Jesus had attacked this attitude head-on with his command of enemy love.[31] The

---

31. Luke's story of the Good Samaritan (10:25-37) makes the same point. John Donahue, "Who Is My Enemy?: The Parable of the Good Samaritan and the Love of Enemies," in Swartley, 137-156, sees the parable as a challenge "both to the historical reality of viewing the Samaritan as enemy and the deeper religious attitude that divides the world into outsiders and insiders." The "dehumanized" foreigner acts according to the scriptures which the lawyer professes to follow and provides an unexpected model of love of neighbor. He also picks up the tab!

command was new and radical both in its absoluteness and in the motivation that grounded it. The two evangelists agree on the basic points. Their accounts also leave several questions unanswered or in doubt.

(1) Neither makes a clear and explicit distinction (though other biblical texts do) between the love owed to fellow disciples and to those outside the community of believers. Certainly the latter are not ipso facto enemies. Just whom Jesus had in mind is not so clear. Luke's enemy seems more generic: haters, cursers, abusers both physical and verbal, beggars, borrowers, "sinners," the ungrateful, the selfish and thieves or robbers (twice). Matthew has some of these, too; but he also refers to persecutors, legal adversaries, tax collectors, Gentiles, the unjust and those who would impose forced labor. Most of these look like outsiders. In both cases the disciple is not to adopt the tactics and attitudes of the enemy.

(2) The love that is enjoined is not mere passivity in the face of hostile behavior or attitudes. Nor is it an emotion. It is a positive and active attitude of generosity and good will, which is described as praying for, blessing and doing good to the enemy.

(3) Nor is it a question of reciprocity. That is, it is not said to be a tactic for getting the enemy to love you or do good to you in return. Luke in particular stresses this point, apparently in response to the pagan reciprocity ethic. It does not seem to be a question of "justice" either. And there is no mention of hope that the enemy will be won over to belief by such loving behavior. The command to pray for him may include this in some indirect way, but this is not stressed.

(4) There will be a reward, but this is not specified except to say that it will come from God. And imitation of God is the primary motive. Enemy love is certainly not a counsel for achieving or practicing self-perfection, in the manner of the Stoics, for example. It is an attitude that should flow from the gift which God has first given. And, besides, God loves his enemies -- another unusual idea in the Bible.

(5) Finally, there is a thread, mostly implicit and assumed, running through the texts and connecting love of enemies with generosity to the poor -- by the poor. Solidarity with the neediest members of the community was something which both Jews and Christians traditionally demanded of themselves. The new connection seems to be that this generosity and solidarity are now to be extended to everyone, including hostile outsiders. This is a heavy demand,

especially for people who themselves had only the barest necessities.

JESUS' TEACHING AND THE OPTION FOR THE POOR

Is this all there is to enemy love: just do it and leave the rest to God? Is there no recourse against injustice? Are there not "objective" evils which in extreme cases (gratuitous killing of loved ones, for example) can only be resisted by force? Might not doing so actually be an act of love toward the aggressor as well as toward the loved one? Jesus seems not to have asked these questions, not in these texts at any rate. In practice, he himself did not resist his executioners. He warned Peter that those who take the sword will perish by it; and he died praying that God would forgive his killers. Is this meant to be a policy for everyone? For all times? Let us examine three recent attempts by engaged Christian scholars to deal with these questions.

(1) Richard Horsley tries to get behind these gospel texts to the original life situation of Jesus' words.[32] He argues that the examples point primarily to personal relations in the conditions of local Palestinian peasant communities: severe economic hardship, people in debt and not able to repay, begging and "some people at each other's throats, hating, cursing, and abusing" (90-91). There was a huge gap between rich and poor; there were taxes, tribute, tithes and unemployment. And there was no doubt a good deal of resentment of the rich minority on the part of the poor majority (91). But, according to Horsley, Jesus was not calling for political resistance or revolution. He was not even thinking primarily about relations with the exploiting classes (Romans and their clients, Jewish religious leaders). Rather, he says:

> these sayings . . . call people in local village communities to take economic responsibility for each other in their desperate circumstances. Those addressed may have little or nothing themselves. But they are called upon to share what they have willingly with others in the community, even with their enemies or those who hate them. (91)

---

32. "Ethics and Exegesis: 'Love your Enemies' and the Doctrine of Nonviolence," reprinted in Swartley (72-101) from JAAR (1986). See too his *Jesus and the Spiral of Violence* (San Francisco: Harper & Row, 1987). Horsley describes himself as a pacifist and practitioner of nonviolence out of religious conviction (Swartley, 97, n. 15).

In Horsley's view, Jesus' focus was not on earthly justice or
general nonviolence or pacifism in any modern sense but on the
coming of the Kingdom and how it was to be brought about in the
conduct of his poor followers in their everyday relationships with their
equally poor neighbors. Still, he claims, this kind of enemy love had
larger implications from the start, for

> when the people have achieved such solidarity with regard to the
> supreme values of life [in this case sheer survival] focused on
> concrete social-economic relations . . . it has usually been highly
> threatening to the ruling groups. The movement gathered around
> Jesus appears to have been no exception. (92-93)

Horsley also wrestles with the problem of the contemporary
ethical relevance of these texts, rooted though they are in the
conditions of a very specific time and place and in a theological-
eschatological context that is strange to modern ways of thinking. He
suggests four possibilities: (a) They might challenge us to think about
and act to realize social and economic conditions based on the kind of
solidarity and mutual care which Jesus enjoins. (b) They might serve to
remind the rich and powerful among us of what the rest of the gospel
says about "Caesar's decree of tribute from subject people, Herod's
'massacre of the innocents,'[33] the inability of the intellectuals and
ruling groups to respond to the coming kingdom, and the passage
concerning why (and by whom) Jesus was crucified" (94). (c) Though
these texts do not require, or even allow, North American Christians to
urge nonviolence on our oppressed neighbors in other countries, they
do underline once again the fact that "Jesus also calls for an
identification with the poor and a voluntary humility, relinquishment
and sharing by the wealthy and powerful (and educated)." (d) While
these sayings, especially the concrete examples, are not necessarily to
be taken literally as universal ethical principles, they do hold up enemy
love as an ideal and that ideal is expressed in terms of social and
economic structures.

(2) Walter Wink belongs to the long tradition of committed
Christian readers who find a more literal and immediate relevance in

---

33. The story of the "holy innocents" was a favorite theme of popular preaching in
Nicaragua during the Contra war. Herod stood for American power; the innocents
were the people of Nicaragua.

the love command.[34] He begins from the question of justice: "To ask the poor and powerless to acquiesce in injustice when that is all they have ever known is itself an act of complicity in injustice . . . Jesus never intended anything of the sort" (103). What Jesus did intend, he argues, is neither violent revolution nor passive acceptance but an imaginative form of active nonviolent resistance of the type practiced by Gandhi, Martin Luther King, Dorothy Day and others.

In this reading, which depends mostly on the Matthean version, "turn the cheek" in response to the insult implied in a (backhanded) slap is a tactic for the oppressed, for whom retaliation would be suicidal. It says, in effect, "Try again . . . I deny you the power to humiliate me. I am a human being just like you. . . You cannot demean me" (105). The oppressor is thus robbed of his power to dehumanize his victim, and the victim gains in self-respect.

"Let him have your cloak as well" is advice to a poor debtor dragged into court because he cannot pay. Rather than be stripped of his dignity he is to strip himself literally and walk out of court naked. He was going to lose the case anyway; the system was rigged against him. In this scenario he avoids shame and at the same time registers a dramatic protest. "Jesus provides here a hint of how to take on the entire system in a way that unmasks its essential cruelty and to burlesque its pretensions to justice, law and order" (108).

Wink maintains that "going the extra mile" is aimed at the hated Roman military occupation. Revolt is neither possible nor desirable. The solution is to regain the initiative, "to liberate themselves from both servile actions and a servile mentality" (111). It is a kind of defiance aimed at baffling the oppressor and empowering the oppressed.

Lending and giving without expectation of return is a practical program of "radical egalitarian sharing" (112) aimed at resisting the conqueror's divide and conquer strategy. Poor peasants, driven to the wall by debt and taxes, tend to become suspicious of and isolated from one another in their need to look out for themselves. This only helps their masters to pick them off one by one. If they stick together that becomes impossible.

---

34. "Neither Passivity nor Violence: Jesus' Third Way (Matt. 5:38-42 par.)," a revision of his paper in SBL Seminar Papers (1988), in Swartley, 102-125. Horsley and Wink respond to one another's essays in Swartley, 126-136. Wink is from South Africa and has been active in the anti-apartheid movement there.

In conclusion, these texts

> form the charter for a way of being in the world that at last breaks
> the spiral of violence . . . [Jesus] articulates, out of the history of
> his own people's struggles, a way by which evil can be opposed
> without being mirrored, the oppressor resisted without being
> emulated, the enemy neutralized without being destroyed.(117)

(3) Luise Schottroff sees an explanatory parallel between the love
command (and other texts) in Matthew and Paul's advice to the early
Christian community at Rome[35]:

> Bless those who persecute you; bless and do not curse. . . Do not be
> haughty, but associate with the lowly. . . Repay no one evil for evil.
> . . Never avenge yourselves, but leave it to the wrath of God; for it
> is written, "Vengeance is mine, I will repay, says the Lord." No, "if
> your enemy is hungry, feed him; if he is thirsty, give him drink; for
> by so doing you will heap burning coals upon his head" [Proverbs
> 25:21-22]. Do not be overcome by evil, but overcome evil with
> good. Let every person be subject to the governing authorities. For
> there is no authority except from God. (Rom 12:13-13:1)

Paul in his preaching -- and the Jews before him -- had known
persecution for the faith, and he fully expected that it would come at
Rome. Roman policy was to allow free practice to other religions but
also to demand occasional tests of loyalty to the official state cult
(sacrifices to the Emperor and the like). These tests, Paul assumes
(though he does not say so here), were to be resisted, thus inviting
persecution. Meanwhile, Christians, who had neither political nor
social-economic standing or power, were to go along with the
legitimate claims of the state. Paul assumes (but again does not say so
here) that even unjust power can serve God's purposes. Besides,
political power is borrowed and not destined to last much longer; and
God will reckon up the accounts.

Likewise, in their personal relations Christians are to follow the
demands of Jesus to love and do good to their hostile neighbors,
especially the "lowly," and not to return evil for evil. Paul understands

---

35. "'Give to Caesar What Belongs to Caesar and to God What Belongs to God': A
Theological Response of the Early Christian Church to Its Social and Political
Environment," in Swartley, 223-257.

such behavior as a "prophetic" announcement of God's love and the coming Kingdom. If the enemies do not respond to it, then they will have condemned themselves. And God will surely punish them, for God is also just. The Christian is not to take vindictive pleasure in this fact, but it is a fact.

Schottroff interprets nonresistance and enemy love in Matthew 5:38-48 in the light of what Paul says here and what the evangelist says in 26:47-56 about Christ's attitude during the Passion. Matthew's examples of nonresistance to evil -- coat and cloak, the extra mile, and turn the cheek -- are to be taken literally, she claims, and not simply as symbols of all possible forms of hostility. Each is a concrete case of injustice, and passive acceptance is not what Jesus meant. The point (though it is not explicitly made) of inviting the aggressor to double his injustice is the same as that of heaping coals of fire on his head in the letter to the Romans. It is "an action of prophetic judgment which expresses the idea that God's judgment is going to catch up with you" (231). On the other hand, loving the enemy, interpreted as praying for the persecutor, is a way of confronting him with an example of God's love and mercy in the hope that he will change his ways and recognize the coming of the Kingdom. This is a paradox, but no less so than the claim that God is both just and merciful. Jesus seems to have held for both.

Schottroff takes the account of Jesus' arrest in Matthew 26:47-57 as a commentary on 5:38-48 and an indication of his stance toward the power of the state, as well as a model for his followers. In general, Matthew thought that the power of Rome and the local authorities in Palestine was unjust and oppressive and that Pilate had Jesus killed for political reasons, though he knew that he was innocent (27:24). For his part, Jesus demanded loyalty to Caesar ("Render to Caesar. . ." [Mt 22:21]), and he did not resist arrest, torture or execution. When Peter cut off the ear of the servant of the high priest, Jesus told him to desist, "for all who take the sword will perish by the sword" (26:52). Schottroff sees this as a reference to God's eventual punishment of all who practice violence (233). Thus the position of Jesus toward the civil authorities is essentially that of Paul in Romans: loyalty to the state, no violent resistance even to injustice and leaving judgment to God.

Some Conclusions and Some Questions

Modern Christians, for the most part, are not conscious of themselves as living near the end of history. The imminent coming of God's Kingdom in justice is not a controlling consideration. Nor do most of us, at least in the United States, live a subsistence peasant way of life under the domination of foreign or domestic oppressors. If anything, we belong to and share in the benefits of an imperial power. Many of us in the so called First World enjoy religious freedom as well as some measure of social, economic, political and intellectual power and privilege. Our societies, while far from perfect, can scarcely be labeled as systemically unjust -- though some would do so. On the other hand, we can hardly claim, either at home or abroad, that we have reached definitive solutions to the problems of hatred, vengeance, personal and institutionalized violence or the oppression of the poor and weak by the rich and powerful.

How then can these texts speak to us, who claim to follow Jesus at such a distance in time and circumstances -- and even in "theology"? They cannot, of course, answer directly all the questions we would like to put to them. Thus, there will always be some disagreement about how to apply them. It seems to me, however, that several things are clear and that it might be helpful to state them by way of summary:

First, there is little doubt that Jesus preached love of enemies and nonretaliation against violence, and this to poor and oppressed people.

Second, in his life, passion and death he practiced what he preached and gave an example for his followers.

Third, at the same time, he believed in God's justice: that there would be righting of wrongs and punishment of violence in God's own time, in God's own way, at the coming of the Kingdom.

Fourth, in our evidence Jesus does not seem to have explicitly addressed the question (as Walter Wink does) of how you get these two things -- nonviolence and justice for the poor -- together. Paul solved it in Romans 12 with his "Vengeance is mine . . . says the Lord . . . if your enemy is hungry, feed him; if he is thirsty, give him drink . . . " God is just, but Christians must be openhandedly generous to their needy enemies and leave judgment of them to God. I think that Luise Schottroff makes a good case for believing that this was also how Jesus would have answered the question. The parable of the wheat and the tares (Mt 13:24-30) seems to point to the same conclusion.

Fifth, Jesus' examples of turning the cheek, going the extra mile and giving the coat as well as the cloak are taken from everyday life, although they would hardly happen every day. In the context, they sound to me more like a rhetorical device aimed at underlining the seriousness of the enemy love/nonretaliation command than suggestions about practical strategies either of nonviolent resistance (Wink) or prophetic denunciation (Schottroff). That is to say, the notion and spirit of doubling the injury in reverse seems to me to be the main point of these examples. What effect this will have on the offender Jesus simply does not say. In the context, he is interested only in its rightness for the believer.

Sixth, Jesus did not speak in precisely the categories used by modern pacifists and advocates of nonviolence. Still, as far as I can see, his words and actions leave no room for violence -- not even in self-defense or for the sake of promoting justice. Total nonviolence is the ideal. And, as the early Christians soon concluded, the demand to live at peace with one's personal enemies contains a presumption against participating in wars. In addition, there are Jesus' warnings about greed and power, which are the roots of war.[36]

Seventh, Jesus clearly cared about the poor and oppressed members of his own society. He lived among them; he shared their lives and took their side. He also made hard demands on them: not only did he forbid them to use violence against their oppressors; he also told them to be generous in lending and giving alms to their equally poor enemies. This fact suggests the following questions, with which I shall conclude this paper:

(a) Given Jesus' teaching and its social and economic context, how can modern, reasonably well-off North American Christians not feel challenged not only to share from our abundance but to simplify our own lives and even to adopt forms of voluntary poverty?

(b) Much less, how can we -- as we are sometimes tempted to do -- think of the needy person only as someone who wants what we have, and hence as in some sense an "enemy"? (I have in mind Jesus' words about giving and lending even to enemies and the hesitation bordering on hostility that I often feel at the approach of a beggar on the street.)

---

36. On the question of Jesus' attitude toward the state, Suzanne Shanley reminded me of Dorothy Day's remark that if Christians were really to "render to God the things that are God's," there would be nothing left over for Caesar.

5.

Thoughts on Personal Wealth

Peter Perkins[37]

Now that we live in a global community, our neighbors include the poor all around the world. What then ought we to do about sharing the wealth of this community with our poor neighbors? My paper focuses on a personal aspect of the question of shared wealth and the balance between accepted affluent life styles and real concern for the poor.

Discussions of options for the poor often move rapidly into support for one ideology or another. In his book *Religion, Wealth and Poverty*, for example, James Schall, S.J., plugs democratic capitalism and decries the thrust of social justice movements which transfer control of the economy away from the people, thus strengthening the state.[38] The poor are not poor because the rich have unjustly accumulated more than their share of the global wealth, Schall claims. Rather, the poor are poor because they have not yet learned how to

37. Peter Perkins received his Ph.D. in Mathematics from the University of California at Berkeley and has published several research papers in the area of mathematical logic. He has taught at Holy Cross since 1962 and served as Associate Dean of the College, Coordinator of Grants and Research, and Departmental Chair. His current interests include mathematical models for notions common to science and religion.

38. See James V. Schall, S.J., *Religion, Wealth and Poverty* (Vancouver: Fraser Institute, 1990).

produce wealth. On the other hand, advocates abound for various shades of socialism with the underlying assumption that the wealthy *have* exploited the poor and that some form of redistribution of wealth is essential.[39]

We who are outside the fields of social philosophy, ethics and economics may not feel competent to defend a particular approach to social justice. But each one of us *is* an authority on our own personal conscience as it reflects on the moral and ethical issues of the day. Rather than attempting to examine systemic weaknesses in governmental and social structures which affect the plight of the poor, this brief paper is more a litany of unanswered personal questions, "true confessions," and an invitation to shared concern over how we use our personal wealth. I leave aside the extremely important questions of what our personal commitment of time and energy should be and of how new resources we might uncover can *best* be used.

The grim statistics on world poverty are so familiar to us that, unfortunately, they no longer seem to have much shock value. According to Oxfam-America's figures for the last decade[40]:

1. More than one billion people are chronically under-nourished.

2. Fifteen to twenty million people die each year of hunger-related causes.

3. Twenty-five percent of the world population has no access to safe drinking water.

4. Eighty percent of the land in eighty-three countries is controlled by three percent of the land owners (and presumably a smaller percent of the total population).

5. More than half of the world's inhabitants cannot read or write.

6. Poor countries have nearly seventy-five percent of the world population but consume only fifteen percent of the world's available energy.

7. North Americans spend more on chewing gum, tobacco, and alcohol than the entire annual budgets of many poor countries.

And on and on. Now obviously, the mere distribution of available

---

39. See John C. Haughey, S.J., *The Holy Use of Money* (Garden City, NY: Doubleday, 1986).

40. See Gary E. McCuen, ed., *World Hunger and Social Justice* (Hudson, WI: Gary E. McCuen Publications, 1986).

goods and services to indigent people will go only so far in alleviating long term suffering. Problems of adapting economic systems to cultural traditions and of chaos produced by political, ethnic and military rivalries, must be solved. It is just as obvious, however, that without material aid from wealthy nations, private organizations, or large numbers of individuals the situation would worsen. All of us who are not poor, have by definition some personal wealth. How we use our wealth is only one part of our "mark in life." How we use our talents is just as important, and clearly we must assign some of our wealth to developing those talents and providing enough relaxation to maximize their use. Surely, finding joy in life is as important as making purposeful sacrifice. But excessive consumerism, for example, is neither a (real) joy nor is moderating it a (real) sacrifice. The obvious question remains. Are we as individuals doing enough? How should we live our lives relative to sharing personal wealth?

I am not able to give satisfactory answers here, but let me briefly examine our potential for sharing and the apparent inertia of our affluent lifestyles. In attempting to do so, and in reflecting on my own life, I cannot avoid the conclusion that many of us are embedded in, addicted to, and unconscious of our own affluence to the point where any expressed "concern for the poor" seems at best inconsistent and at worst almost hypocritical.

Both my wife and I were raised in middle class families in Vermont in the 1940's-50's with no special inclination toward materialism. As an idealistic college student, I even entertained the idea of living a Spartan life in one form or another. In fact, I actually approached this state as a married graduate student and for a while as a college instructor with two young children -- clearly not in the sense of real poverty but at least having to make significant sacrifices so that ordinary bills could be paid. Gradually, because my wife was able to work as a school psychologist, we progressed toward a middle class status again. Somehow, with good luck, two wage earners when one was the norm, and a reasonable economy, we continued to climb the economic ladder. Even though we increased our family size through three adoptions, we were in the thick of middle class consumerism.

During this time, as I now analyze it, we were "driven" by several factors: first, a natural desire to provide the best opportunities we could for our children; second, fear of a future time in old age when we might have no means of support; third, a desire (perhaps unconscious) to return to and improve on the middle class status of our childhood; and fourth, an acceptance of a more materially self-indulgent life style almost as compensation for whatever time and energy we spent on others.

We pursued the American dream, not, I would say, in the crass sense and not without sacrifice. Nevertheless, in that process we became materially better off than ninety-eight percent of the rest of the world. My conscience has given its approval for the most part, but now at midlife I am beginning to hear from my "conscience checker" or second-level conscience. This new voice is asking me why I now spread expensive chemicals on my lawn three or four times a year to make the grass more green instead of settling for a yellow-green color when millions of people spend their entire existence trying to get enough food from the land to barely survive on? Do we need three television sets and four telephones for two of us and our dog, when so many are without simple communications? Do I need to drive a Subaru, this voice is asking, when I could just as well drive an Escort and give the $3000 difference to a good cause? Do we need to add a master bathroom to our home when hundreds of millions do not even have clean drinking water? In fact, now that the children have left, why do we need a ten-room house at all when there are thousands of homeless within just a few hundred miles? My conscience has somehow given what I would call C-minus responses to all of the above questions; my "conscience checker," however, proposes a failing grade. The sad part is that although I am aware of the near hypocrisy of the situation, I will most likely be unable to disengage from these residual excesses.

I suspect many of you also have a dormant conscience checker. When it is finally allowed to speak, it may acknowledge the heavy burden of paying for a college education but then go on to ask: Do I really need to spend $800 on spring break to get the rest I must have when many have never taken a vacation in their entire lifetime? Will getting that fifth pair of jeans, that tenth blouse and skirt, or that state-of-the-art CD player really help me enjoy life more? Do I need two J. Crew jackets and $700 worth of alcohol each year to be the "socially accepted person" I want to be?

It is not that you and I are heartless or unmoved by suffering. I am sure we all have given that cup of water to the thirsty stranger. But what about the other ten who have yet to drink? We all pay taxes, a good portion of which does go to entitlement programs; we all make contributions to the United Way or other charities. But many of us still have enough left to buy boats or stereos or second homes or expensive educations. It is true that as consumers we are creating jobs; but would not that also be the case if we pooled some of our expendable income and built low cost housing, or financed start-up businesses in poor neighborhoods?

As a mathematician, I tend to try a reductionist approach to understanding everything; but it is clear even to me that no philosophical or theological system will ever give us a complete set of moral norms for living in the affluent society. My luxury may be your necessity; your emotional needs may be incomparable to mine. As with so many other moral questions, we find ourselves unable to give definitive answers, which is another indication of the weakness of the human condition. On the other hand, we are, as a global civilization, progressing to higher levels of consciousness, and this movement, I believe, is accompanied by a deeper and more perceptive collective conscience. My hope is then, that our students, as future affluent young people, will struggle with these questions at an earlier age before they become unconsciously and irreversibly attached to the habit of accepting all the amenities that they can reasonably afford.

Granted, moderating our lifestyles to create *new* resources for self help projects is a small and, indeed, not very exciting option among the many we have for the poor. But it would seem to me impossible to choose even this option without also modifying our attitudes, which is exactly what is necessary for a more comprehensive attack on poverty.[41]

41. I also consulted the following titles in preparing this paper: Joseph F. Gower, ed., *Religion and Economic Ethics* (The Annual Publication of the College Theology Society, Vol. 31, 1985; London: University Press of America, Inc., 1990); Harold S. Kushner, *When All You Ever Wanted Isn't Enough* (New York: Pocket Books, 1986); and Redmond Mullin, *The Wealth of Christians* (Maryknoll, NY: Orbis Books, 1984).

COMPARING THE STATE OF CHILDREN

1960   1990

....

Children born to unmarried mothers:
5%   28%

....

Children under 3 living with one parent:
7%   27%

....

Children under 3 living with both parents:
90%   71%

....

Children under 3 living with a divorced parent:
2%   4%

....

Children under 18 experiencing the divorce of their parents:
less than   almost
1%   50%

....

Mothers returning to work within one year of a child's birth:
17%   53%

....

Children under 18 living in a one-parent family (approximately)
10%   25%

....

Infant mortality (deaths before first birthday)
28/1000   9/1000

....

Children under 18 living below the poverty line:
27%   21%

....

Married women with children under 6 years old in the labor force:
18.6%   60%

....

Source: Carnegie Corporation Report; U.S. Census Bureau; The Urban Institute; National Center for Children in Poverty. Cited in *The New York Times*, April 12, 1994. Copyright (c) 1994 by The New York Times Company. Reprinted by permission.

6.
Childhood Poverty:
Sociology and the Option for the Poor

David M. Hummon[42]

Thus the sociological problem is not so much why some things "go wrong" from the viewpoint of the authorities and the management of the social scene, but how the whole system works in the first place, what are its presuppositions and by what means it is held together. The fundamental sociological problem is not crime but the law, not divorce but marriage, not racial discrimination but racially defined stratification, not revolution but government.

-- Peter Berger, *An Invitation to Sociology*

Peter Berger (1963) once defined a sociologist as "someone concerned with understanding society in a disciplined way." Though this portrait, like all rapid sketches, runs the risk of caricature, it does highlight several distinguishing features of the sociologist. First, sociologists are first and foremost theorists, not practitioners. Their primary goal is to produce *knowledge* about society, knowledge which

42. David M. Hummon is an Associate Professor of Sociology. In addition to interests in the sociology of childhood, he has published work on American culture and community life, including recent articles on place identity and community attachment.

is often as useful to sinners as to saints. Second, sociologists study *society* -- its organization, institutions, and culture -- not the individual. Of course, sociologists do study individual men and women, but sociologists do so to investigate how social forces are fateful for the lives of these individuals. Finally, sociologists are committed to *empirical research* -- disciplined inquiry that involves the direct observation of human action rather than speculation about how human action ought to be. In doing so, sociologists adopt norms of scientific inquiry, including commitments to objectivity and verifiability.

Given such predilections, what can the sociologist contribute to discussions of the option for the poor in the context of Catholic higher education? On overcast days, I might well be inclined to answer "not much," for the option's emphasis on ultimate values and religious and political action does not translate well to disciplinary commitments to theory and research. On sunnier days, I am inclined to answer "a good deal," for sociology's disciplined study of society promises insights into poverty that are not otherwise available. Such intellectual clarity -- involving both empirical analysis and a distinct social vision -- is valuable, both as a way of opening our vision to an option for the poor and as a basis for possible action as citizens and Christians.

To illustrate this claim, I will examine a number of ways that contemporary sociologists think about poverty in general and the poverty of children in particular. The specific focus of this essay arises in part out of personal interests. As a parent and citizen, I have become concerned with the well-being of children in our society. These personal interests in turn have shaped my professional work, and I have begun to teach and write about American children. Yet, this personal interest is also expressive of a troubling social fact: children are disproportionately likely to be poor in our society. Of poor Americans in 1990, more than 40% were children under 18, although children make up only 27% of the population. This means that more than one in five children under eighteen were poor, a rate that increases to one in four among children under six years of age (Children's Defense Fund, 1992). Perhaps most disturbing is that after a significant decrease in the rate of childhood poverty between 1959 and 1979, poverty among children has been rising during the last decade and a half (Bianchi, 1990).

1. CHILDHOOD POVERTY AS A SOCIAL PROBLEM: CULTURE AND IDEOLOGY

If asked to consider childhood poverty as a social problem, I might begin by noting that the extent to which poor children are regarded as a social problem is itself a social phenomenon, a phenomenon influenced not only by the extent of material deprivation among children but also by a culture's conceptions of both childhood and poverty. Such a theoretical emphasis on social definition is not an exercise in moral relativism; I believe that our society's neglect of its children is wrong. Rather, it is expressive of my commitment as a sociologist to analyze society, a commitment that involves the frank recognition that common-sense understandings of "the problem" may themselves need scrutiny.

For example, with respect to our conceptions of childhood, I believe the poverty of children is regarded as problematic not only because it involves the material deprivation of a human being but also because it involves the deprivation of a *child*. As Americans, we conceive of childhood as privileged status -- a separate and protected stage of life, at once happy and free and dependent (Cunningham, 1991). Childhood poverty thus offends because it violates our conception of what childhood *ought* to be. Such a social valuation of childhood is a relatively recent accomplishment in the cultural history of the West, particularly with respect to poor children. As Cunningham (1991) has documented, children of the poor at the end of the 17th century in England were regarded as different from children of the rich, and *properly different*. Their poverty was hardly problematic: the only question was how to prepare them for a life of labor suitable to their station in life. Not until the 19th century in England and the United States (Zelizer, 1985) was the middle-class conception of childhood as a privileged stage of life -- exempt from labor, valued in terms of sentiment rather than productivity -- extended to children of the poor. Such sacralization of childhood itself constituted a profound cultural transformation of the meaning of childhood, a transformation accomplished through political action and social conflict (Zelizer, 1985).[43]

---

43. In this context, it is worth noting that Jesus' identification of the Christian self with childhood constituted a radical departure from the cultural attitudes toward children of the day (Sommerville, 1990, esp. 49-61). His sympathy for children, in contrast to the cultural idealization of childhood of the modern period, was a sympathy for the oppressed.

In a similar fashion, cultural conceptions of poverty -- of its causes and moral significance -- also mediate the way we think about childhood poverty. As Wuthnow (1993) has recently noted, Americans are profoundly ambivalent about wealth and poverty. On the one hand, in a nationally representative sample of employed adults, most citizens (92%) agree that the condition of the poor is a serious social problem, and many are highly critical of American materialism: 89% affirmed that "our society is too materialistic"; 74% percent said "materialism is a serious social problem." On the other hand, three-out-of-four (78%) of these same Americans report desiring material abundance ("a beautiful home, a new car, and other nice things"), and they especially admire those who have attained wealth. Thus, 80% say they admire "people who make a lot of money by working hard," compared with 69% of Americans who say they admire a person who takes a lower paying job to help others or 60% who admire a person who works hard but never makes much money. Relatively few Americans (12%) believe it is wrong to want a lot of money.

As a sociologist, I would interpret these ambivalent views by placing them in the context of America's culture of individualism, a shared way of thinking that is more likely to interpret wealth or poverty in terms of *individual achievement* than *social structure,* including the on-going system of class inequality itself. For example, when the general populace is asked to explain poverty, more often than not they point to the personal attributes of individuals than to social structural causes, or for that matter, to fate. In 1980 the majority of Americans regarded lack of thrift (64%), effort (53%), and ability (53%) as very important causes of poverty, substantially more than those who attributed poverty to low wages in some industries (40%), the failure of private industry to provide enough jobs (31%), prejudice or discrimination against blacks (31%), or bad luck (12%) (Kleugel and Smith, 1986). Such individualistic interpretations of inequality are typically combined with a moral individualism that distinguishes between the "deserving" and "undeserving" poor, reserving approval for those individuals who are poor by accident of fate (the blind), stigmatizing those who are poor by assumed lack of effort ("the bum"). In doing so, individualistic beliefs function socially as a class ideology, at once explaining wealth and poverty in terms of individual effort and legitimating inequality -- whatever its causes and scope -- in terms of a moral calculus that honors "achieved wealth" and stigmatizes the undeserving poor.

The ideological consequences of the culture of individualism for the politics of inequality are at once profound and complex. For instance, with respect to children, individualistic beliefs obscure the simple fact that 40% of America's poor -- children -- are hardly poor because of lack of thrift, effort, or ability. Few children have failed to achieve in the market place since they are for the most part excluded from economic activity, nor for that matter have they had much opportunity to choose their parents and their attendant class position in society. Cultural distinctions between deserving and undeserving poor do, however, tend to valorize the poverty of children. Nevertheless, such an individualistic frame of reference often works against the interests of poor children by stigmatizing their parents as undeserving poor (e.g., the "welfare mother") and by undermining the political viability of structural solutions to childhood poverty. For instance, as I will note below, the rise of childhood poverty in the 1980's was partially due to reductions in the value of governmental aid to mothers with dependent children (AFDC), reductions that were politically legitimated in terms of cuts to "undeserving" parents, however disastrous such cuts were to the well-being of "deserving" poor children.

2. EXPLAINING CHILDHOOD POVERTY: SOCIAL STRUCTURE AND INSTITUTIONS

In thinking about childhood poverty, sociologists are not only interested in analyzing (and often critiquing) popular conceptions of poor children; they also work to discover the social causes of poverty among children. Such an endeavor is difficult. As we have just seen, "common-sense" interpretations of such matters are inevitably inadequate: they reflect, in their ideological biases, the very problem they purport to interpret. Moreover, social reality is highly complex. To confront these difficulties, sociologists rely on systematic empirical analysis, a theoretical perspective that emphasizes social structure and institutions, and an ongoing debate within the discipline that challenges the adequacy of conflicting interpretations. Taken together, these efforts produce a complex picture of the social causes of childhood poverty, a portrait that includes facets of social organization (class, race and gender) and institutions (the family and the state).

(A) INEQUALITY, CLASS, AND POLARIZATION

Sociological interpretations of the causes of poverty typically begin, not with poverty itself, but with inequality. However important material deprivation is, it is only part of the story, for poverty, like wealth, is part of a larger system of social stratification. Such stratification involves the unequal distribution of a society's resources, including wealth, power and social prestige. How unequal is U.S. society with respect to economic life?

Wealth, as measured by ownership of property and assets, is highly concentrated. In 1983, the richest fifth of the population held nearly 80% of the wealth; the top one-half of one percent of all families is estimated to own 35% of all wealth. Moreover, after long-term declines in the concentration of wealth from the 1920's to the 1970's, wealth appears to be becoming more concentrated in the last decade and a half (Schaefer and Lamm, 1992).

Income, though not distributed as unequally as wealth, is distributed quite unequally. In 1989, the top fifth of the nation (with incomes of $45,224 or more) received 47% of wages and salaries; the bottom fifth (with incomes of $11,417 or less) received less than 4% of the income. Income among the top fifth is, moreover, quite concentrated. The richest 5% of American families receives a larger share of the nation's income than does the bottom 40% of American families.

How does such inequality compare with other societies? On the one hand, cross-national and historical comparisons of income inequality indicate that all advanced, industrial societies have distributions of income that are more egalitarian than agrarian, less economically developed societies. On the other hand, when compared with other industrialized countries, United States income equality is relatively unequal. For instance, in Japan the top 10% of families received 2.4 times as much income as the bottom 20% of families; in the United States, the ratio was 4.4 (Farley, 1990). Moreover, there is considerable evidence to suggest that income, like wealth, has become somewhat more unequally distributed during the last decade and a half, largely because the earning power of middle and working class Americans has been eroded. This change, caused to a large extent by structural shifts in the economy from high wage industrial jobs to lower wage high tech and service jobs, has increased the polarization of American family income with two middle-income families falling in economic position for every middle-income family that moved up in rank (Eitzen and Zinn, 1993).

Such patterns of economic stratification among adults are reflected in economic status of American children in a number of important ways. Clearly, the degree of concentration of wealth and income among the American families means that other American families go without, and that the children of those families suffer the consequences of that material deprivation. Moreover, the relative inequality of American society translates directly to relative inequality among children. A recent comparative study of childhood poverty in wealthy industrial countries indicated that the United States, the richest of the six countries studied, had the highest poverty rate among children. In 1979, the U.S. rate for children was 17.1; for Australia, 16.9; the United Kingdom, 10.7; Canada, 9.6; West Germany, 8.2; Sweden, 5.1 (Smeeding and Torrey, 1988). Perhaps most tellingly, the recent polarization of income inequality can be documented for the well-being of American children. Over the last two decades, such structural changes as the elimination of industrial jobs and the erosion of minimum wage by inflation have meant that working class families have had increasing difficulty of avoiding poverty even while working (Children's Defense Fund, 1992). Such economic trends have increased the over-all rate of poverty among children. However, not all children have suffered during this period. While the income of poor children declined absolutely in the 1980's, the income of the richest children grew rapidly, widening the gap between the wealth and poverty of American children (Lichter and Eggebeen, 1993).

(B) THE EROSION OF GOVERNMENT SUPPORT TO FAMILIES WITH CHILDREN

The poverty of American children is not only shaped by the place of their parents in the American class system; the state, through direct and indirect programs, also influences the well-being of America's children, including its poor children. Both the extent and consequences of such political action are complex; yet, a number of facts are important for a basic understanding of childhood poverty.

First, the government is directly involved in defining the poor through its Official Poverty Index ($13,359 for a non-farm family of four in 1990). Currently, 35 million Americans live in poverty, approximately 13.5% of the population. This definition is consequential both for public perception of U.S. poverty and for the administration of public policy. As an absolute measure of poverty, based on money income necessary to purchase basic food, this measure does not indicate changes in relative poverty, i.e., changes in the different proportions of income received by rich and poor. Thus it does not call attention to increased polarization in the class structure (Lichter and Eggebeen, 1993). Its use of *one* indicator of poverty (namely, food costs) is also inadequate. As a pre-tax and transfer indicator, it inflates the poverty rate to some extent; by not including housing costs, which have escalated much faster than food costs over the last three decades, it deflates the poverty rate significantly (Bane and Ellwood, 1989).

Second, government tax and transfer benefits do help to reduce the poverty of children. In 1979, for instance, such transfer payments reduced the childhood poverty rate from 16.9 to 13.8. Nevertheless, in a comparative study of six industrial societies, U.S. government transfers were the least effective in reducing childhood poverty. In fact, because U.S. programs are relatively ineffective compared to those in England, Canada, Germany, Australia, Sweden, and the United Kingdom, post-tax and transfer poverty rates are actually more unequal between countries than pre-tax and transfer rates (Smeeding and Torrey, 1988). Two factors make U.S. programs relatively ineffective compared to programs elsewhere. Poor children in the United States are considerably less likely to receive *any* benefits from government transfer programs than are children in other countries. Amounts of income aid to poor children, both in real dollar terms and as a proportion of gross domestic product, are *lower* in the U.S. than other countries (Smeeding and Torrey, 1988).

Finally, government programs to help children such as AFDC and food stamps decreased in effectiveness during the eighties. For instance, while the median monthly state AFDC payment provided poor families with an income equivalent to 71% of the poverty line in 1970, by 1992 median AFDC payments provided families with children a payment equivalent to 41% of the poverty line. This meant that such transfer and in kind payments, which had enabled one in five otherwise poor families to escape poverty in 1979, only enabled one in eight to do so in 1991 (Children's Defense Fund). This pattern of declining support for children contrasts sharply with the role of government programs to aid the elderly. Poverty rates for elderly Americans declined sharply from 1959 to 1979 (35.2% to 15.2%), and they have *continued to decline* in the eighties to a low of 12% (Bianchi, 1990). Such differential impacts of government action on the elderly and the young indicate that poverty rates are partially the outcome of political power and institutional policy.

(C) FAMILY STRUCTURE, RACE, AND POVERTY

Much debate about childhood poverty has focused on issues of family structure, particularly the role that changes in family structure over the last three decades may have played in the well-being of children. Three interrelated changes are particularly notable. First, American families are becoming smaller, with the average number of children per family declining from 2.33 in 1970 to 1.81 by 1988 (Bianchi, 1990). Second, children are increasingly likely to live in single-parent families. In 1960, 9% did so; by 1988, 24% lived with one parent, nearly always the mother (Bianchi, 1990). Such single-parent families have become more frequent both because of increasing divorce and non-marital fertility. Between 1950 and 1980, the divorce rate more than doubled, and in any given year the number of children who see their parents divorce more than tripled from six per thousand children to eighteen per thousand (Bianchi, 1990).

Increases in non-marital fertility are even more dramatic. In 1960, 5% of children were born out of wedlock; by 1987, 25% of all children were born out of wedlock. Moreover, while such rates have risen dramatically for both white and black Americans, non-marital fertility rates are much higher for blacks: 62% for blacks; 17% for whites in 1987. Third and finally, during the last decades, women have been increasingly likely to work outside the home for pay, resulting in increasing proportions of children with a mother in the labor force. For instance, in 1970, 39% of children under 18 and 29% of children under six had employed mothers; in 1988, the figures were respectively 62% and 53%. Such increases in the participation of women in the labor force have been most dramatic in two-parent families, as participation rates in mother-only families have historically been high. For example, by 1970 53% of single-parent mothers with children under 18 were already in the labor force (Bianchi, 1990).

How have these changes affected the economic well-being of children? On the one hand, it is clear that children in single-parent families are much more likely to be poor than children in two-parent families (54% versus 10% in 1988), and that the increasing incidence of single-parent families has contributed to the rise in poor children. Specifically, Eggebeen and Lichter (1991) estimate that "child poverty rates would be one-third less in 1988 if family structure [with respect to one versus two-parent families] had not changed since 1960." Moreover, their analysis indicates that the increasing divergence in family structure between blacks and whites also exacerbated inequality in poverty rates between black and white children. By 1988, for example, 14.6% of white children were poor, 37.9% of Hispanic children and 44.2% of black children (Bianchi, 1990).

On the other hand, increased labor force participation of women and declining fertility exerted downward pressure on children's poverty rate. This means that poverty rates would have been even higher had not families reduced their size and spouses entered the labor force. However, such economically beneficial impacts for children were uneven. Most of the accrued benefit to children of mother's employment was gained in the 1960's and 70's, and it went largely to children of dual-career families. The combined impact of these countervailing trends was a further polarization of the well-being of children, with white children in two-parent, dual-career, relatively small families doing relatively well, and black children in single-parent families becoming poorer.

These insights into the demographic sources of childhood poverty raise a final question that deserves explicit comment. To the extent that increased childhood poverty is partially due to the increased frequency of single-parent families, why are single-parent families more likely poor? The obvious answer -- that such families are likely to have only a single income as opposed to two-parent households -- is in fact true; but as Bane and Ellwood (1989) have argued, it is only part of the story. First, poverty is itself one of the causes of family disruption: that is, poor two-parent families are more likely to become single-parent families than are well-to-do, two-parent families. Second, most children in single-parent families still have two living biological parents, but only the custodial parent contributes significantly to their support. The non-custodial parent, nearly always the father, typically provides little support to the child; nearly two out of three absent fathers provide no support for their children. Third, since single-parent families are nearly always female-headed, these families also suffer from gender inequities in wages. When such single-parent working women are black Americans, they also face inequities in wages due to racial inequality. In short, the relative impoverishment of children in single parent households must also be understood in terms of the social *consequences* of poverty, the sexism of legal institutions that exempt absent fathers from child support, and the sexism and racism of economic institutions.

CONCLUDING COMMENTS

What, then, of the option for the poor and education at Holy Cross? What does this sociological analysis suggest? Certainly, one lesson I have hoped to convey is the seriousness of poverty among children. We are not doing well by many of our children, nor are we supporting poor and working-class parents in their struggle to provide for their families. In comparative terms, we have done better as a nation in the recent past, and there is considerable evidence that other societies, with equal or fewer resources, are providing more adequately for their poor children. Such material deprivation causes immediate and long-term suffering for children of the poor. They are more likely to die in the first year of their life, to have continuing health problems, to receive inadequate health care, to experience family disruption, to get in trouble with the law, and to leave school early (Eitzen and Zinn, 1993: Schaeffer and Lamm, 1992).

A second lesson is that we are not likely to do better for our children unless we think critically and carefully about issues of children and poverty. Popular views of these issues fail to grasp the social causes of childhood poverty because they suffer from the ideological biases of class interests and individualistic culture. Here, colleges, and particularly colleges that explicitly make poverty a matter of critical inquiry and debate, can prove useful as a setting for reasoned discussion of these difficult matters. Here, colleges that offer students and faculty opportunities to work with poor children can prove useful as a mechanism for challenging popular attitudes toward the poor.

A final lesson is that we are not likely to do better for our children unless we address the structural and institutional sources of childhood poverty. In saying this, I do not mean to imply that individual service to poor children is unworthy of effort. It is, as an act of compassion and of justice. However, if sociologists are correct in suggesting that childhood poverty is rooted in class inequality, that it is compounded by inequities of gender and racial stratification, that it is exacerbated by eroding families and supports for those families, then childhood poverty cannot be addressed simply as a matter of individual reform or service. The implications of this lesson for colleges are less clear if one believes, as I do, that there are useful limits to the extent to which colleges can become directly involved in organized social or political action. Nevertheless, I am sure that we can do better for our children and that to do so we will need to work together, as citizens and concerned Christians, to improve the very workings of our local communities and national institutions. In this sense, the problem is not so much the material poverty of children as the communal and spiritual poverty of a society that insures the deprivation of a significant portion of its children.

References

Bane, Mary Jo and David T. Ellwood. 1989. "One Fifth of the Nation's Children: Why Are They Poor?". *Science* 245: 1047-1053.

Berger, Peter, 1963. *An Invitation to Sociology*. New York: Doubleday Anchor.

Bianchi, Suzanne M. 1990. "America's Children: Mixed Prospects." *Population Bulletin* 45 (1): 1-42.

Children's Defense Fund, 1992. *The State of America's Children*. Washington, D.C.

Cunningham, Hugh. 1991. *The Children of the Poor: Representations of Childhood Since the Seventeenth Century*. Oxford: Blackwell.

Eggebeen and Lichter, 1991. "Race, Family Structure, and Changing Poverty Among American Children." *American Sociological Review* 56:801-817.

Eitzen, D. Stanley and Maxine B. Zinn. 1993. *In Conflict and Order: Understanding Society, Sixth Edition*. Boston: Allyn and Bacon.

Farley, John E. 1990. *Sociology*. Englewood Cliffs, N.J.: Prentice-Hall, Inc.

Feagin, Joe R. 1975. *Subordinating the Poor: Welfare and American Beliefs*. Englewood Cliffs: Prentice-Hall, Inc.

Kluegel, James R. and Eliot R. Smith. 1986. *Beliefs About Inequality: Americans' Views of What Is and What Ought to Be*. New York: Aldine de Gruyter.

Lichter and Eggebeen. 1993. "Rich Kids, Poor Kids: Changing Income Inequality among American Children." *Social Forces* 71 (3): 761-780.

Schaefer, Richard and Robert Lamm. 1992. *Sociology*, 4th Edition. New York: McGraw-Hill, Inc.

Smeeding, Timothy and Torrey, 1988. "Poor Children in Rich Countries." *Science* 243:873-77.

Sommerville, C. John. 1990. *The Rise and Fall of Childhood*. New York: Vintage Books.

Wuthnow, Robert. 1993. "Pious Materialism: How Americans View Faith and Money." *The Christian Century* (March 3): 238-42.

Zelizer, Viviana. 1985. *Pricing the Priceless Child: The Changing Social Value of the Child*. New York: 1985.

God has destined the earth and all it contains for the use of everyone and of all peoples, so that the good things of creation should be available equally to all, with justice as guide and charity in attendance. Whatever forms property may assume, adapted to the legitimate institutions of peoples according to differing and changing situations, attention must always be focused on this universal destiny of goods. For this reason, in making use of them, *we ought to regard the exterior things we lawfully possess not just as our own but as common, in the sense that they can profit not only the owners but others also.* However, *everyone has the right to have a part of these goods that is sufficient for each and his or her dependents.* This was the view of the fathers and doctors of the church in teaching that we are obliged to support the poor, and not just from our surplus. *A person who is living in extreme need has the right to procure from the riches of others what is necessary for personal sustenance.* Since so many in the world are crushed by hunger, this holy council urges everyone, individuals as well as authorities, to be mindful of the view of the fathers, "Feed those who are dying of hunger, because if you have not fed them you have killed them", and actually to share their goods and make them available according to their ability, especially by providing individuals and peoples with aid which can enable them to help and develop themselves.

-- Vatican II
Gaudium et Spes, #69

76

7.
Option Versus Options for the Poor:
Selected Economic Issues

Charles H. Anderton
David K. W. Chu[44]

When Jesus said, "The poor will always be with you" (Mt 26:11), he did so in the context of a lavish use of wealth for something other than helping the poor. There is enough material in this one account to keep academics from a wide variety of disciplines discussing and debating what is meant by "option for the poor." We take "the poor will always be with you" as a call to be continuously involved in a perpetual problem.

As economists, we approach the notion of the option for the poor with some trepidation. Economists are by nature relativists. We do not mean relativists in the moral sense, but relativists in the material sense. The iron law of scarce resources and goods, which never will be repealed in this world, imposes material relativism. Resources devoted to one activity are not available for use elsewhere. Individuals must decide how they should allocate their scarce resources to produce the

---

44. Charles H. Anderton teaches international economics, economics of conflict, and principles of economics at Holy Cross College. His research specialities are the arms trade, arms race modeling, and defense conversion. David K. W. Chu teaches cost accounting, nonprofit accounting, and principles of accounting at Holy Cross. His research interests are the financing of health care systems, hospital financial reporting and cost analysis, and the economic behavior of private nonprofit organizations.

economic goods which satisfy their needs and desires. Judas was thinking in these terms when he thought that the ointment lavished upon Jesus could have been sold and the money given to the poor -- or to himself (Jn 12:1-6).

Material relativism leads most economists to view proposed solutions to social problems in shades of gray rather than in black and white. The impassioned reformer who has taken up some particular cause, such as environmentalism, will be quite exasperated by the agnostic economist who is wont to say, "Allocating more resources to clean up the environment is likely to leave less resources for other important areas."

Material relativism in economics, however, does not mean the absence of priorities. Poverty is of great concern to economists because the primary (and some would say the only) purpose of an economic system is to provide a wide array of material options for as many people as possible. Economists are not concerned only with the distribution of goods. We are also very interested in the size of the economic pie to be distributed. However, the way in which the pie is distributed has a significant influence on the size of the pie itself. Both the distribution of the pie and its size, among other things, influence the extent of poverty in a society.

The first moral duty of anyone interested in fighting poverty is to think clearly about its causes and the conditions of its prevention. This has been expressed well by the economist Kenneth E. Boulding (1968: 190-191):

> This [concern for social ills] is a most proper motivation, yet it needs to be disciplined by a strong sense of scientific integrity and by a willingness to acquire real skill in the abstract disciplines before venturing to make applications. Our notions of what *ought to be* must not be allowed to prejudice our painstaking inquiry into what *is*, and goodwill is in no sense a substitute for scientific competence. . .

The second moral duty is appropriate action. Boulding warns that a person can become "so engrossed in the refinements of scientific abstraction -- and in the substantial rewards -- that he forgets the ills of society and becomes deaf to the cry of the hungry and blind to the misery of the oppressed." (Boulding 1968: 191). The story of a graduate school dean who wondered whether there might be some research money to be made for the school if his faculty undertook research projects on poverty is an apt illustration of Boulding's point.

There are, then, two errors that must be guarded against. A Type 1 error is action without having thought clearly, even theoretically, about the complexity of poverty. A Type 2 error is an in-depth theoretical understanding with little or no action. Economists often maintain that non-economists are prone to Type 1 error. Many non-economists believe that economists are prone to Type 2 error. Could we both be right?

Diversity of viewpoints is not a bad thing. What is most puzzling, however, is that those with different views often arrive at opposite conclusions based on much of the same empirical evidence available. Different presuppositions, ideological commitments and approaches may be important explanations of this phenomenon. Perhaps the proverbial story of the blind people and the elephant is pertinent. Is it possible that those holding diverse viewpoints about the causes of and solutions to poverty have grasped only part of the truth? Is the part sometimes mistaken for the whole? Could not those prone to Type 1 and Type 2 errors have struggled towards a synthesis that would have done greater justice to the complexity of poverty and led to a more accurate and balanced treatment?

In this paper, we illustrate a few of the ways in which economists teach their students about poverty. We focus on poverty in the U.S., though some of the issues are also relevant to poverty outside of the United States. A principles of economics course cannot provide an in-depth treatment of poverty; what it can do is give students a taste of the complexity of poverty and an awareness that the way it is portrayed by the popular press is often superficial.

FOUR ECONOMIC PRINCIPLES FOR EXAMINING POVERTY

From an economist's standpoint, the phrase "option for the poor" means the following: *every public policy must be examined, first and foremost, on the basis of its impact on the poor.* The reason for considering the poor first is that, unlike the rich and the middle class, poor people do not possess many resources and will therefore be most adversely affected by the negative impact of any policy -- good intentions of the policy-makers notwithstanding. Economic thinking is structured within a framework characterized by several major principles. We discuss four principles which are relevant to this paper in that they provide us with a basic framework to examine poverty.

1. *Every scarce good has a cost -- nothing is "free."* A scarce good is obtained only by giving up some other scarce good. For example, if time is spent watching an exciting football game, that same

amount of time cannot be used for serious studying in the library. "Free" elementary education is provided through tax money paid by the area's residents. Moreover, the resources used to build an elementary school could have been used to produce other facilities, such as public housing. One has to be given up for the other.

2. *Individuals choose purposefully -- they economize* (in the economist's language, they are "rational"). People do not deliberately waste their valuable resources. Given their own limited resources, they will choose options which best advance their personal objectives as they see them. For example, if faced with two options that give equal satisfaction, a person will choose the option with the lowest cost. Likewise, if faced with two options of equal cost, a person will choose the one which gives the most satisfaction. Pursuit of personal objectives is not necessarily selfish. For example, it is in Mother Theresa's self interest to purchase medicines for her patients at the lowest possible cost. We suspect that she "shops around" to make the most of the resources with which she has been entrusted.

3. *Human choice is influenced by changes in economic incentives: their choices are predictable.* A person will more likely choose an option when personal benefits derived from choosing that option increase. Conversely, a person will be less likely to choose an option the costs of which is expected to increase. Although many other factors also determine how people make decisions, economic incentives will always remain a powerful influence.

4. *The secondary effects of a policy must be considered -- they are as important as the primary effects.* The initial impact of a policy is usually just the tip of the iceberg. Other factors indirectly related to the initial policy might also have been affected. Their impact can only be seen or felt after a period of time. For example, rent controls will reduce the amount spent on rental units, but it might also discourage new production of apartment complexes and lead to deterioration of existing ones. A severe apartment shortage could arise in the longer run where only those with "connections" will be able to get units.

DATA ON INCOME: INCOME DISTRIBUTION

Many people's understanding of poverty begins with a look at the *income inequality*. Income inequality can be observed in every society. In a market economy, each person's income is determined by what they receive from others in exchange for their products. People differ in their productive abilities, opportunities, preferences, and personalities. Those who produce things highly valued by others will receive high incomes. Others with few skills may have difficulty just supporting themselves. How much inequality is there in the U.S.? Table 1 shows the share of *before-tax annual money income* received by quintile -- a quintile is each fifth of families ranked from the lowest to the highest income. If annual income were equally distributed, each quintile of the population would have received 20 percent of the aggregate income. Although Table 1 shows an unequal distribution of income, the trend is towards greater income equality from the 1930's to 1970. Since 1970, however, income inequality appears to have increased.

Table 1.
INEQUALITY IN THE MONEY INCOME OF FAMILIES, SELECTED
YEARS

PERCENTAGE OF BEFORE-TAX AGGREGATE MONEY INCOME RECEIVED BY:

	Lowest 20 % of Recipients	Second Quintile	Third Quintile	Fourth Quintile	Top 20 % of Recipients
1935-36	4.1	9.2	14.1	20.9	51.7
1950	4.5	12.0	17.4	23.4	42.7
1960	4.8	12.2	17.8	24.0	41.3
1970	5.4	12.2	17.6	23.8	40.9
1980	5.2	11.5	17.5	24.3	41.5
1985	4.7	10.9	16.8	24.1	43.5
1989	4.6	10.6	16.5	23.7	44.6

(Source: Bureau of the Census, cited in Gwartney and Stroup, 680.)

To gain a better understanding of this inequality, one must examine the factors which influence income distribution. Table 1 alone is an insufficient basis for drawing conclusions because of the information *left out*. First, it does not differentiate family size, age of the income earner, and the number of earners in each family. For example, although college students and retirees typically earn much less than people in their prime working years, and are thus in the lower quintiles, they are not "poor" as we understand the term to mean.

Second, Table 1 was based on income *before* taxes. Taxation is a way of taking resources from the top quintile and giving it to bottom quintile. Families in the lowest quintile receive these benefits in non-cash form (food stamps, health care, housing). Browning and Johnson

(1979) examined income distribution *after taxes and non-cash transfers*. They found a substantial reduction in income inequality. The top quintile received about *eight times* the amount of the lowest quintile before taxes and non-cash transfers. After taxes and non-cash transfers were factored into the computation, the top quintile received about *four times* the annual income of the bottom quintile. Furthermore, Table 2 seems to refute the popular impression that the higher income quintiles paid less taxes in the 1980's relative to the lower income quintiles:

Table 2.
THE CHANGE IN FEDERAL INCOME TAX REVENUE DERIVED FROM
VARIOUS INCOME GROUPS, 1981-1988

Tax Revenue Collected from Group
(in billions of 1982-1984 dollars)

Income Group	1981	1988	Percent Change 1981-88
Top 10 percent of Earners	150.6	199.8	+32.7
Top 1 percent	55.9	96.2	+72.1
Top 5 percent	110.5	159.2	+44.1
All Other	161.8	149.1	-7.8
Total	312.4	348.9	+11.7

(Source: U.S. Department of Treasury, cited in Gwartney and Stroup, 119.)

We must therefore look beyond the data in Table 1 for more information. Table 3 outlines the major differences in the characteristics of high- and low-income families:

Table 3.
THE CHARACTERISTICS OF HIGH- AND LOW-INCOME FAMILIES,
1989

	Lowest 20% of Recipients	Highest 20 % of Income Recipients
Average years of schooling (Head of Household)	10.3	14.7
Age of Household Head: (Percent Distribution)		
Under 35	36.0	14.0
35-64	40.0	78.0
65 and over	24.0	8.0
Family Status:		
Married-couple family (Percent of total)	52.0	94.0
Single-parent family (Percent of total)	48.0	6.0
Persons per family	2.93	3.41
Earners per family	0.82	2.31
Full-time earners per family	0.37	1.84
Percent of married-couple families in which both spouses work	30.0	78.0
Percent of total weeks worked supplied by group	7.0	31.0

(Source: U.S. Department of Commerce, cited in Gwartney and Stroup, 681.)

We see several things: (1) high income recipients were better educated; (2) they were more likely to be in their prime working years; (3) they were more likely to be married-couple families in which both spouses earn income; and (4) they worked over four times as many weeks as low income families in 1989. These findings lead to the

84 Option for the Poor

conclusion that the increases in income inequality since the 1970's may
have many causes. The following are some possibilities.

1. Compared to the late 1960's and early 1970's, the 1980's
witnessed more single-parent families and more dual-earner families.
We illustrate the problem with two hypothetical families -- the Wongs
and Chans. In 1970, both families were in the middle income group,
each with two children and one wage-earner making $30,000 (in 1990
dollars). In 1990, the Wongs are divorced and Mrs. Wong, who has
custody of the children, is working part-time to provide for her family.
It is very likely that the single-parent Wong family of 1990 will drop to
the lowest quintile of the income distribution table. In contrast, both
parents of the Chan family of 1990 work outside of the home and each
earns an annual income of $30,000. It is now equally likely that the
dual-income Chan family will rise to the top quintile of the same
income distribution table. In other words, a mere change in family
structure exacerbates income inequality.

2. Earning differentials between skilled and less skilled workers
have increased in recent years. Table 4 shows widening income
differentials between workers with different levels of education as we
moved from the 1970's to the 1980's. The world is a dynamic place.
We have entered an era in which other countries have become much
more competitive than before. Under such competitive pressures, the
minimum level of skills U.S. workers needed to earn a good living in
the 1970's can no longer suffice for the 1980's.

Table 4.
INCREASING EARNINGS DIFFERENCES ACCORDING TO
EDUCATIONAL ATTAINMENT.

	Percent that Median Income of College Graduates Exceeds Median Income of High School Graduates		Percent that Median Income of High School Graduates Exceeds Median Income of Persons with 9 to 11 Years of Schooling	
Year	Males	Females	Males	Females
1974	27	54	27	34
1980	35	63	40	39
1984	49	74	50	41
1986	60	93	48	43
1988	53	89	51	55

(Source: U.S. Commerce Department, cited in Gwartney and Stroup, 684.)

INCOME MOBILITY

We now move beyond the issue of income inequality to the issue of *income mobility*. Given that people are classified along an income continuum, an interesting and important question is whether the same people remain in those same categories over the years. In other words, we want to examine the question, "Do the rich stay rich and the poor stay poor?"

To gain some insight into answering this question, we begin with Table 1 again. Table 1 presents what economists call "static" information; it is like a snapshot presenting a situation at a moment in time. In Table 1, people are grouped according to their income levels based on data collected at the end of a particular year. What Table 1 fails to show is the "dynamic" aspect of people and their income levels. What we mean is the ability of people in low income groups to increase their earnings from one year to the next, and concomitantly, the inability of people in high income groups to sustain their earning levels. The movement of people across income groupings is termed *income mobility*.

Table 5 shows the income groupings of families in 1984 relative to the income groupings of *those same families* in 1980. We see clear indications of income mobility in a period of only four years. Only 62 percent of the highest income families in 1980 sustained their status in 1984. Some of them had dropped to the lowest income category by 1984. Similarly, 64.5 percent of the lowest income families in 1980 remained in that category in 1984. Some of them had risen to the highest income group by 1984. The greatest amount of mobility can be seen in the middle income groupings (second, third and fourth quintiles).

Table 5.
INCOME MOBILITY: FAMILY INCOME RANKING IN 1984
COMPARED WITH RANKING IN 1980.

Family Income Quintile, 1984

Family Income Quintile, 1980	Highest	Second	Third	Fourth	Lowest	Total
Highfest	62.0	23.6	8.4	3.7	2.3	100%
Second	26.6	36.9	23.6	8.9	4.0	100%
Third	6.0	26.5	35.8	23.4	8.3	100%
Fourth	4.0	9.3	24.0	41.9	20.8	100%
Lowest	1.4	4.0	8.0	22.1	64.5	100%

(Source: Institute for Social Research, University of Michigan, cited in Gwartney and Stroup, 687.)

The conclusion we draw from income data must be done with the utmost caution. Static data, such as the income distribution data of Table 1, hide the fact that many high income families had much lower incomes just a few years before; and families with low incomes had attained much higher incomes in previous years. Thus people exchange relative economic positions over time. The rich do not necessarily stay rich and, likewise, the poor do not necessarily stay poor.

We hope this brief discussion illustrates the idea that using simple income distribution data is not necessarily revealing. Although the income distribution data (Table 1) may show apparent inequalities, the data conceal many things (such as non-cash benefits, changes in family structure, income mobility) which surface only after further investigation.

POVERTY RATE

Having examined some pitfalls in the measurement and uses of income data, we can now discuss how they are related to poverty. The government publishes annual statistics on poverty. The most visible poverty datum is the "poverty rate." How is this statistic derived? Each year, the government collects information from a sample of 60,000 households that are representative of the entire U.S. population. A family whose *money income* falls below a predetermined level is defined as poor. The percentage of these families in relation to the total

60,000 households is termed the *official* poverty rate of the year.

The key to understanding the poverty rate is to know the threshold money income level below which a family is defined as poor. The method for deriving this threshold income level was developed by the Social Security Administration in 1964. At that time, data showed that low- to median-income families of three or more persons spent about one third of their income on food. The poverty threshold income was thus set at *three times the cost of an economical and nutritionally adequate food plan* (this threshold is adjusted for family size and price level changes over the years). Since 1964, however, *non-cash benefits* (food stamps, health care, housing) targeted for low income families have grown rapidly. Using money income data to calculate the poverty rate may exaggerate the problem because it fails to include these various benefits which accrue to low income families. Economists are more comfortable with the *adjusted poverty rate* which is derived by including the cash value of those non-cash benefits in family income. For example, the adjusted poverty rate was 8.8 percent in 1989 compared to the official poverty rate of 10.3 percent.

GOVERNMENT ANTI-POVERTY EFFORTS

Regardless of how it is measured and presented, poverty is a problem that cannot be ignored. The U.S. government began an ambitious program to fight poverty in the mid-1960's. The conventional wisdom of the time was expressed in the *1964 Economic Report of the President* (excerpt taken from Gwartney and Stroup 1992: 691):

> Conquest of poverty is well within our power. About $11 billion [about $44 billion measured in 1990 dollars] a year would bring all poor families up to the $3,000 income level we have taken to be the minimum for a decent life. The majority of the nation could simply tax themselves enough to provide the necessary income supplements to their less fortunate citizens. The burden -- one fifth of the annual defense budget, less than 2 percent of GNP -- would certainly not be intolerable.

The period 1965-1975 witnessed a rapid growth of government income transfer programs. These transfers were targeted both at the elderly and the poor. Table 6 presents data on the history of overall government transfers and Means-Tested Transfer Payments (specific transfers to the poor, i.e., persons or families whose income falls below the poverty threshold) since 1965. The data in Table 6 show a consistent increase in the amounts and proportions of Means-Tested Transfer Payments. Measured in 1987 dollars, the $102 billion spent in 1987 was almost *quadruple* the amount spent in 1965 ($28 billion). *In relation to personal income*, those same amounts were 2.7 percent in 1987 compared to only 1.5 percent in 1965. As for total transfer payments (including payments to the elderly), 1987 payments comprised 19.4 percent of personal income compared to 8.5 percent in 1965. Clearly, the government has spent large amounts of resources, both in terms of the amounts of money and in relative percentages of personal income, to finance programs for the poor and the elderly.

Table 6.
TRENDS IN GOVERNMENT INCOME TRANSFERS, 1965-1987

Year	Total Transfer Payments as a Percent of Personal Income	Means-Tested Transfer Payments	
		Total (Billions of 1987 dollars)	As a Percent of Personal Income
1965	8.5	28.0	1.5
1975	17.4	79.6	3.0
1980	17.8	90.3	2.9
1987	19.4	102.0	2.7

Includes non-cash transfers such as food stamps, school lunch subsidies, public housing and other housing subsidies, Medicaid, and Medicare. (Source: *Economic Report of the President: 1991*, Department of Commerce, cited in Gwartney and Stroup, 692.)

The government has been spending money on these transfer programs for almost thirty years since they began in 1965. Assessing the poverty rates in light of these spending programs is the next logical step. Table 7 shows various official poverty rates for the period 1947-1989. Ironically, the sharpest declines in poverty rates for all age groups were in the years prior to 1965 -- *before* the government's "war on poverty." Since 1965, poverty rates have not dropped dramatically. The rate dropped from 13.9 in 1965 to 10.0 in 1968. Since then, poverty rates have stayed at the 10 to 11 percent range. This trend is particularly disturbing in light of the large government spending to combat poverty in this same period.

Table 7.
OFFICIAL POVERTY RATES, 1947-1989

Year	Official Poverty Rate (all age groups)	Official Poverty Rate (elderly families)	Official Poverty Rate (non-elderly families)
1947	32.0	N.A.	N.A.
1959	18.5	30.0	16.6
1965	13.9	22.8	10.9
1968	10.0	17.0	9.0
1975	9.7	8.9	9.8
1980	10.3	9.1	10.5
1985	11.4	7.0	12.2
1989	10.3	6.6	11.0

N.A. = Not Available. (Source: Department of Commerce, cited in Gwartney and Stroup, 692-693.)

We gain more insight into this phenomenon when we separate the poor into two groups: elderly (aged 65 and over) and non-elderly (under age 65). We now see an important difference in their respective poverty rates. The poverty rate for elderly families, i.e., families presumably in retirement, generally declined during the period 1959-1989. However, the poverty rate for non-elderly families, i.e., working-age families, bottomed in 1968 and rose throughout the 1970's and early 1980's. Their poverty rate in 1989 (11.0%), after twenty-four years of government assistance, is almost identical to their rate in 1965 (10.9%) when the programs were begun.

Why these phenomena of greatly increased government spending and stubbornly stagnant poverty rates? Table 8 shows significant changes in the characteristics of the poor. In 1959, 57 percent of the poor were headed by people in their prime working years; 70 percent of the poor worked at least some part of the year; and 23 percent of poor families were headed by a female. In 1989, however, 77 percent of poor families were headed by people in their prime working years; only 49 percent of the poor had worked at least some part of the year; and 52 percent of poor families were headed by a female.

Table 8.
CHARACTERISTICS OF THE POOR AND THE POVERTY RATES OF
SELECTED GROUPS: 1959, 1976, AND 1989.

	1959	1976	1989
Number of poor families (in millions)	8.3	5.3	6.8
Percent of poor families headed by a:			
Female	23.0	48.0	52.0
Black	26.0	30.0	31.0
Elderly person (aged 65 and over)	22.0	14.0	10.0
Prime working age (25-64)	57.0	72.0	77.0
Person who worked at least some during the year	70.0	55.0	49.0
Poverty rate:			
All families	18.5	10.1	10.3
Married-couple families	15.8	7.2	5.6
Female-headed families	42.6	32.5	32.2
Whites	16.5	8.1	7.8
Blacks	54.9	32.2	27.8
Children (under age 18)	26.9	14.9	19.0

(Source: Department of Commerce, cited in Gwartney and Stroup, 691.)

These statistics show a strong association between *family instability* and *poverty rates*. Association does not infer causality. One can argue for the possibility that family instability causes poverty just as strongly as one's argument for the vice versa. Regardless of which position is taken, the fact remains that, contrary to expectations, government income transfers appear to have been a relatively ineffective weapon against non-elderly poverty. This is where an analysis of the *secondary effects* of a government policy is necessary. We believe income transfers may have effectively helped some of the poor, but also severely hurt the welfare of other poor people.

The poor are not homogeneous. Economists distinguish between two groups of poor people: the *hard-core poor* and the *marginal poor*. The hard-core poor are people who are generally victims of debilitating diseases, or physical, mental, or emotional disabilities. They have little means for recovery and remain poor throughout the good and bad times. On the other hand, the marginal poor are people who are there because of job loss, change in marital status, premature termination of schooling, or early pregnancy. The marginal poor still have the ability to make choices which will impact how often they become poor and how long they stay poor. Government transfer programs do not necessarily impact the marginal poor positively because of negative secondary effects. We discuss two of these secondary effects:

    1. Transfer programs reduce the incentives to earn money. Table 9 illustrates this problem:

Table 9.

THE EFFECT OF TRANSFER BENEFITS AND TAXES ON THE INCENTIVE OF A PENNSYLVANIA MOTHER WITH TWO CHILDREN TO EARN INCOME (SEPT 1983)

Annual Gross Wage	Transfer Benefits	Income and Employment Taxes	Spendable Income	Implicit Marginal Tax Rate%
$--0--	$7,568	$--0--	$7,568	--
$2,000	6,525	134	8,391	58.8
$4,000	5,482	268	9,214	58.8
$5,000	3,040	346	7,694	252.0
$6,000	2,059	611	7,448	124.6
$7,000	1,719	810	7,909	53.9
$8,000	1,378	1,021	8,357	55.2
$9,000	1,038	1,240	8,798	55.9
10,000	698	1,469	9,229	56.9

(Source: U.S. House of Representatives Committee on The Ways and Means, cited in Gwartney and Stroup, 695.)

    Line one shows the initial state of a Pennsylvania mother with two children: no gross wage, $7,568 in transfer benefits (includes welfare check, the monetary value of food stamps, and the equivalent monetary value of "free" health care), and thus spendable income of the same amount. Suppose this mother obtains a job and earns $2,000 in annual gross wage. We move to line two. She still qualifies for welfare but obtains the lesser amount of $6,525 in transfer benefits because of her employment status (food stamps are reduced, for instance). In addition, her gross earnings are now subject to a $134 income tax. Consequently, this mother's spendable income is now $8,391 ($2,000 + $6,525 - $134). At this point, one might argue that she is better off getting the job because $8,391 (line two) is more money than $7,568 (line one).

The result, however, is misleading. The key is *additional spendable income in relation to additional gross income*. By earning $2,000, her spendable income does increase from $7,568 to $8,391 -- an $823 increase. However, she has had to earn $2,000 in order to generate this $823 increase. The $2,000 earned did not result in a direct dollar for dollar increase in spendable income. Otherwise, spendable income would have increased by exactly $2,000. Her employment status resulted in reduced transfer benefits and increased taxes, both of which reduced the increase in her spendable income to only $823.

In other words, although she earned an additional $2,000, she only received $823 in spendable income -- the rest ($1,177) was "taxed" away in the form of reduced benefits and increased taxes. Economists call this an "implicit marginal tax." For line two, the amount of implicit tax was $1,177 and the implicit marginal tax rate was 58.8 percent ($1,177 ÷ $2,000). As we can see in Table 9, the implicit marginal tax rate rises and falls as the mother earns more money, but it stays consistently above 50 percent. If this mother earns $5,000 in annual gross wages (line 4), the implicit marginal tax rate is 252 percent. This is like earning $100 in income and paying $252 in "taxes" on that income. Under these incentives, a poor person will be strongly influenced either *not* to get a job, work fewer hours, or work but not report any earnings. For this mother, in addition to "taxes," there is the logistical problem of caring for the children while she is working and the added expense of transportation to and from work.

2. A longer-term (dynamic) effect, perhaps even more pernicious than the high implicit marginal taxes is the lost opportunity to acquire job skills that will lead to higher wages later in life. The marginal poor may subsequently find it more difficult to compete against people who have continued to work in the market place for the same job. These difficulties further prevent them from getting employment. Having been excluded from the work force for a long time, these people become less and less able to support themselves. Finally, they move from being marginally poor to becoming the hard-core poor. As Gwartney and Stroup so succinctly state: "The long-term consequences of an incentive structure that encourages non-work is even more destructive than the short-term effects." (1992: 696).

CONCLUSIONS

Our understanding of the option for the poor is based on the several issues we have discussed thus far. We believe in thinking about the option for the poor in light of the four fundamental economic principles discussed earlier: (1) every scarce good has a cost; (2) individuals choose purposefully; (3) human choice is influenced by changes in economic incentives; and (4) the secondary effects of a policy may outweigh the intended primary effects and thus must be considered.

Although income inequality and poverty exist in every society, the reasons are complex enough that anyone trying to tackle these problems should do so with extreme caution. Income inequality is based on annually published income distribution data. They only show a static situation and do not depict the dynamic movement of people out of one income group and into another. On the other hand, Table 5 shows that income mobility is possible. People in the U.S. have been able to get out of their income group into a higher income group. We saw from Table 5 that 64.5 percent of the lowest income group in 1980 remained in that same group in 1984. This means some of the poor people have been able to improve their financial situation and get out of poverty.

Merely designating government transfer programs as the *only* option for the poor is, we believe, a grave error. We have seen how unresponsive poverty rates have been despite massive government spending of almost three decades. Tables 3 and 8 show us the social characteristics of poverty. Increases in divorce rates and births to unwed mothers have substantially increased the incidence of female-headed households. Given the circumstances of these households, the poverty rate among them is especially high. If there are to be options for them, these options must create a *preventive* incentive; that is, an incentive not to get into a situation that will eventually lead to poverty. Giving poor people welfare money after the fact is not a healthy long-term solution.

We believe government plays an important but not exclusive role in fighting poverty. Rather than just *one overriding option* -- government -- we believe *a set of options* is more appropriate for the poor. First, these options should *empower* the marginally poor so they can climb out of their predicament. To do so, these options should create a set of incentives that would induce people to improve their financial status -- to become self supporting and eventually to become well off. The worst thing a policy can do is permanently to *entrap* the poor in their present conditions. Second, the hard-core poor, who cannot support themselves regardless of the economic incentives, must be given another set of options which provide them with a meaningful and respectable existence.

To expound upon this set of options would be beyond the scope of this paper. We conclude by suggesting a four-pronged approach to fighting poverty. First, government programs are necessary in that they provide a safety net for the hard-core poor. Second, support for the family is crucial in preventing divorce and the resulting instability. A stable family structure is crucial to providing support to people who are in poverty. Third, religious organizations and other charities in local communities tend to be much closer to the "action" and can respond to poverty more directly than can a federal or state bureaucracy. Local institutions will also monitor the effects of their efforts with much more interest because *their* money is directly at stake. Fourth, students can be taught that they can assist the poor in their communities and globally through charitable contributions of time and money. We are fond of Compassion International's motto: "You may not be able to change the world, but you can change the world for one person." We believe a corollary follows: "If you are not changing the world for one person, you are not changing the world."

References

Boulding, Kenneth E. *Beyond Economics: Essays on Society, Religion, and Ethics*. Ann Arbor: The University of Michigan Press, 1968.

Browning, Edgar K. and Johnson, William R. *The Distribution of the Tax Burden*. Washington, D.C.: American Enterprise Institute, 1979. Cited by James D. Gwartney and Richard L. Stroup, *Economics: Private and Public Choice* (Fort Worth: The Dryden Press [6th edition], 1992), 682.

Gwartney, James D. and Stroup, Richard L. *Economics: Private and Public Choice*, 6th ed. Fort Worth: The Dryden Press, 1992.

8.
Not a Private Matter: Pedagogies and Strategies for Institutional Change

Carolyn Howe[45]

What would our society and a Catholic liberal arts college look like if we took seriously the religious call for a preferential option for the poor? What kinds of changes would be necessary at such an institution if the college were to carry out its mission to uphold a preferential option for the poor? I would like to situate these thoughts by presenting the evolution of my own understanding of the concept of the preferential option, and argue that if we want to implement an option for the poor, we have to stop thinking about changing individuals and start thinking about changing institutions. To do this, we need sociological understanding as much as we need theological insight.

My introduction to the preferential option for the poor came about nine years ago when I heard a speaker give an impassioned public lecture about what our society would look like if it adopted such an option. First of all, he said, we would recognize that in a nation as rich

---

45. Carolyn Howe teaches sociology at Holy Cross and specializes in social movement and social change. She is currently doing research on women's community-based activism in the City of Worcester, and is the author of *Political Ideology and Class Formation: A Study of the Middle Class* (Praeger, 1992).

as ours, it is a social and moral scandal that so many people are poor or unemployed or working in jobs that do not allow them to reach their full potential. We would know that when there are people living in mansions, and empty houses are being burned down by landlords for insurance purposes, homelessness becomes a matter of social sin. We would believe that the poor and the most vulnerable of our citizens -- children, elderly, and marginalized people -- have a special claim on our nation's concern. Recognizing all of this, we would work actively to build a more just society. The speaker called for distributive justice, which "requires that the allocation of income, wealth and power in society be evaluated in light of its effects on persons whose basic material needs are unmet." How will a cut in property taxes affect the poorest and most vulnerable children in our school systems? How will cuts in welfare spending affect the largest group of poor people in this country -- the children? If we make a preferential option for the poor, said the speaker, we will support a policy of full employment where every person is guaranteed a job which offers sufficient income to have a decent standard of living and which offers each person the opportunity to feel dignity and self-fulfillment on the job. As a nation, we will establish "a floor of material well-being on which all can stand."

Who was this speaker who made such moving but radical proposals? Some tax-and-spend Democrat? Some leftist activist from the 60's? No. The speaker was Rembert Weakland, the archbishop of Milwaukee, chief author of the U.S. Catholic Bishop's statement, "Economic Justice For All: Catholic Social Teaching and the U.S. Economy."[46]

Throughout the 1960's, 70's, and 80's, Catholic priests and bishops throughout North and South America have been calling on Christians and other moral people to take a stand on the side of the poor, who are demanding social justice in the economic, political, and social institutions of their nations. The Bishops were calling on us to have a "conversion to the poor."

One of the joys of teaching at Holy Cross is that many of our students come to us already convinced that it is important to care about the less fortunate among us. They are already seeking ways to make their personal contribution to justice. In other words, some of us are already converted to the poor. Our task, as educators at a Jesuit

---

46. The United States Catholic Bishop's, *Economic Justice For All: Catholic Social Teaching and the U.S. Economy* (Washington, D.C.: U.S. Catholic Conference, 1986).

institution, then, is to push our students forward and to help them figure out how best to act on their already good instincts. Courses in ethics, theology, and social justice, the First Year Program, and community service programs are indispensable in our curriculum. Such opportunities can help students develop moral and ethical answers to the question, "How then shall we live?"

But these programs are not enough. If students are going to make a moral commitment to the poor, they need to have an accurate analysis. They need a sociological understanding of the conditions which create poverty. They need to gain a deeper understanding of the social structures in our society that privilege some people and dis-privilege or oppress others and learn how they can use their privilege to help bring social justice to the world. It is no accident that one of the six Jesuits murdered in El Salvador (in 1989) was a sociologist whose insights into the workings of the system helped the university carry out its preferential option for the poor with an informed understanding of the society in which the poor lived.

The pedagogical point here is that having an option for the poor is not a private matter. Poverty is not a private matter. Poverty is the result of a system that creates poverty. If we help one person out of poverty either by offering that person a full scholarship or by helping him or her to get a job, we have not done anything about the conditions which continue to create poverty. We need conversion to the poor, yes; but we also need conversion away from charity and voluntary poverty and toward a sociological understanding of the conditions that create inequality.

Students also need to know that opting for the poor carries a price. The Brazilian bishop Helder Camara once remarked that when he gave the poor food, people called him a saint; but when he asked about the causes of their hunger, he was called a communist.[47] In most parts of Latin America, religious people have moved beyond charity to a serious commitment to understanding and challenging the conditions that create poverty in the first place, and have done so at great risk. The six Jesuits murdered in El Salvador were part of this tradition, and they paid with their lives for accepting the fundamental sociological understanding that to help the poor, we must understand the institutions that perpetuate poverty. Even their housekeeper and her daughter were murdered.

47. See Penny Lernoux, *People of God: The Struggle for World Catholicism* (New York: Penguin Books, 1989), 184.

Matters are not much different today. Acts of charity by our students, such as working at the Mustard Seed or tutoring city kids, are generally met with approval. But those students who were asking how the North American Free Trade Agreement (NAFTA) will affect the poorest and most vulnerable in our society and in Mexico, who invited people to sign cards against the NAFTA agreement, were harassed by staff and students alike; some were even called communists. Faculty members who incorporate readings by marginalized people in their courses are often criticized as being "too politically correct."

This brings me to the second level in my evolving understanding of the preferential option for the poor, which could be referred to as "conversion by the poor." This level of understanding developed out of my reading of Black feminist writings and pedagogies for teaching about race, class and gender inequalities. These writings point out the dangers of "exclusionary thinking" and call upon us (the privileged) to make the experiences of previously excluded groups more visible and central in the construction of knowledge. Sociologists and anthropologists are noted for going into poor or marginalized communities to document their observations of the behaviors of the people in those communities. But this new approach would have us turn the camera around to document how "they" see us and the world, while keeping the microphone within the oppressed community in order to record "their" understanding of what they see. We are asked to "re-center our frame of reference," to listen to the voices of marginalized people, not simply to understand those voices but to understand what those voices say about "us."

Jon Sobrino, the Salvadoran Jesuit who escaped being murdered with his brothers four years ago because he was out of the country at the time, says that the option for the poor does not mean to focus on a part of the whole in order to ignore the rest, but rather to reach out to the whole from one part. Sobrino says that the world from the point of view of the poor must enter the university's heart and mind. Does this mean that we abandon the curriculum in favor of "poverty studies"? No; we do not focus on a part of the whole (poverty) and ignore the rest (wealth). Instead, we reach out to the whole, an understanding of how wealth and poverty are related, from the part, which is the point of view of the poor.

What this approach suggests is that by making a preferential option for the poor, we recognize that by looking at the world from poor people's vantage point, we will be able to observe the world more accurately and more thoroughly, without obfuscations. When we look at them, we do not always see an oppressed people. When they look at us, they usually see an oppressor people, and if we listen to their voice, our consciousness may be changed. This is what is meant by conversion "by" the poor. But here again, we need analysis. As educators, we must help both privileged and oppressed students critically analyze the ideologies that inform their own understanding, for too often understanding is confused by the ideologies that deny the structural foundations of inequality. To help the oppressed, we must stop oppression as it operates in the world and allow the structural nature of that poverty to become ever more a part of our consciousness.

This brings me to the third stage in my understanding of the concept of the "preferential option for the poor," which might be thought of as a "conversion to action." Only recently did I learn that the preferential option for the poor carries with it a theological mandate for action. Some theologians argue that the preferential option for the poor means that if God must choose between an oppressed people and their oppressors, God will make a choice -- a preference -- to be on the side of the oppressed, while still loving both the oppressed and the oppressor. Recall the parting of the Red Sea in the Book of Exodus. Which side was God on? Does this story mean that "we" will be swallowed up by our own drive for privilege and power if we fail to take heed of what the oppressed are telling us, what they want, what they need?

As a sociologist, I do not have the background to address the theological meaning of the "option for the poor" in the events of the Exodus. As a sociologist, I do know that if we who are privileged fail to address the problems of the inner city, we will metaphorically be swallowed up by a Red Sea. If we fail to provide a quality education for all of our children, we will pay as a society for our neglect. I do not believe, however, that God will part the Red Sea for South Central Los Angeles, or for the children in the Worcester Public Schools. It makes more sense to me to say that *we* have been given the capacity to create a better society.

God has given us the capacity for moral outrage at injustice, the capacity to understand the conditions that create injustice, and the capacity to take action against social injustice. Many theologians would argue that God acts through us to bring about God's kingdom on earth and it is out of this special responsibility that we are called upon to take a preferential option for the poor and to do so through social action for justice. But we have not used our capacities very well. We are better at loving the poor than we are at listening to them or thinking about why they are poor. Poor people do not need to know that we love them. They need to know that we are giving of ourselves to change the conditions that make them poor. That, ultimately, is a more profound and active form of love. Changing hearts is not enough. We need to change institutions. A book I used in my First Year Program classes last year which had a profound effect on many students was Robert Bellah's *The Good Society*. The students learned that living a good life is not a private matter. It requires having a good society to live in. A good society must be good for all people, inclusive of themselves and their families, the poor, the marginalized, the young, the old, the oppressed. A society that is good for the poor will be good for the non-poor. But the reverse is not necessarily true. An option for the poor is an option for a good society and such a society is in the interests of any moral person who is willing to relinquish the unfair benefits of privilege. To live in a "good society" we have to work collectively to change the institutions that shape our lives.

But just as we do not get rid of the root causes of poverty simply by helping poor people climb out of poverty, neither can we transform the institutions that create unjust conditions by opting out of them. Social action is not a private matter. Social action to bring about social change requires collective action -- working together to create a better society. For this to happen, we must put our students in touch with the traditions that have long worked for social justice and we must give them an analysis of how people transform institutions.

In a provocative article on how the Christian inspiration of the option for the poor can be brought into the university, Jon Sobrino stated the following:

> Far too frequently Christian universities have not questioned a society's unjust structures, nor used their social weight to denounce them, nor have they made central to their work the research and planning of new just models for society. As a matter of fact, by producing professional people who, in most cases, have served to shore up unjust systems, Christian universities have effectively supported the evils of today's world.[48]

Sobrino is telling us that those of us who educate men and women

---

48. Jon Sobrino, S.J., "The University's Christian Inspiration." Translation of article in *Estudios Centroamericanos* (ECA), No. 468, October, 1987. Reprinted in *Companions of Jesus*, 153-54.

to go uncritically into professional jobs may inadvertently help to perpetuate the systemic inequalities that foster human misery and suffering. What is too often lacking for our professional graduates is a conversion "by" the poor, a conversion "to" the poor, and a conversion to action.

A Christian university, says Sobrino, "is one which places itself at the service of the kingdom of God from an option for the poor. This service must be done *as* a university, and even by means of a university's particular nature."[49] Colleges and universities must use their resources to question society's unjust structures, use their social weight to denounce them, and make central to their work the research and planning of new just models for society. Within the context of this academic institution and this city, Holy Cross must make sure that its own policies and structures take into account their effect on the most vulnerable of its students and employees. The College should fund institutes that examine the problems of poverty, health, education and quality of life in our community; it must be prepared to denounce any tax structures and decisions that would deprive Worcester's children of a quality education; it must use its institutional influence on boards of directors of community organizations attempting to create a more just economic, political, and social life in the City. It must develop a curriculum that genuinely converts students, giving them an analysis of the institutional nature of poverty and the collective processes by which institutions can be changed. Holy Cross must be called to solidarity with the people of this community and the world who are in a struggle between life and death; who face economic insecurity; whose jobs deny them dignity or the opportunity to find meaning in our collective lives. In short, if we want to educate men and women "for others," Holy Cross must become an "institution for others."

We must not teach students to pity; they must learn to have compassion. It is not enough that we teach students compassion; we must help them acquire an analysis. It is not enough that we have an analysis. We must use our analysis to empower people. It is not enough that people feel empowered. We must help them to create a good society.

49. Sobrino, "The University's Christian Inspiration," 152.

Our American traditions encourage us to think of justice as a matter of equal opportunities for every individual to pursue whatever he or she understands by happiness. Equal opportunities are guaranteed by fair laws and political procedures -- laws and procedures applied in the same way to everyone. But this way of thinking about justice does not in itself contain a vision of what the distribution of goods in a society would end up looking like if individuals had an equal chance to pursue their interests. Thus, there could be great disparities in the income given to people in different occupations in a just society so long as everyone had an equal chance of getting a well-paid job. But if, as is now becoming painfully apparent, there are more qualified applicants than openings for the interesting jobs, is equal opportunity enough to assure justice? What of the socially disadvantaged for whom a fair race is to no avail since they are left well short of the starting line?

-- From Robert Bellah, et. al., *Habits of the Heart*

9.

Holy Cross' Mission in Light of the Preferential Option for the Poor

Mauri A. Ditzler[50]

Holy Cross' anniversary celebration has been an appropriate backdrop for our ongoing discussions of the "Preferential Option for the Poor." Consistent with the College's traditions, the discussions have drawn heavily from a series of thought-provoking essays by Jesuit scholars. We have wrestled, individually and collectively, with the role of the preferential option principle in our educational mission. Throughout the process, we have been drawn to reflect upon the rich heritage associated with the College's one hundred and fifty years of value-centered education.

Many of us, students and faculty alike, find aspects of the preferential option arguments to be troubling. Stephen Pope, a theologian at Boston College, writes that criticisms of this principle are generally based on an objection to what initially appears to be a call for "unjustifiable partiality or bias in favor of the poor."[51] Pope points out

---

50. At the time of the symposium Mauri Ditzler was the Director of the Honors Program and a member of the Chemistry Department at Holy Cross. He has since been named Dean of the College of Arts and Sciences at Millikin University in Decatur, Illinois.

51. Stephen J. Pope, "Proper and Improper Partiality and the Preferential Option for the Poor", *Theological Studies* 54 (1993), 242.

that in our culture partiality is often associated with "ignorance" and "discrimination." This alone would ensure a careful scrutiny by the academic community of our teaching about the preferential option.

Equally problematic to many at Holy Cross is what appears to be a claim that God shows a preference for one economic class over another in terms of both a greater love and a more complete revelation. Even for those who accept, as does Pope, that the partiality is "morally justified and necessary" the rhetoric and demands associated with the preferential option can seem strident or openly confrontational. Traditional approaches to our responsibilities, as affluent Christians, toward the world's poor are subjected to criticism because they do not proceed from real solidarity with the poor. Championing their causes is not sufficient; we are called to make the cause of the poor our own.

In his widely read essay on the inspiration which should underlie a Christian university in our time, Jon Sobrino suggested that the life-defining demands of the preferential option apply to Christian institutions as well as to individual Christians.[52] He argues that it is in promoting a realignment of the unjust social order that an institution like ours justifies its existence. The traditional way of doing our educational business can actually exacerbate economic inequities. Sobrino goes on to argue that the preferential option for the poor (as a way of working toward the Kingdom of God) provides a focus that can and should serve to unify all activities within the university. That is, it should be the "guiding principle" that ties together various disciplines and the multiple tasks (e.g., teaching and research) of the faculty.

Most of us would object to having our institutional mission so rigorously defined because a liberal arts college draws strength from the diversity of methods and approaches employed across the curriculum. An exclusive focus on the causes of poverty could prove troubling to faculty who are struggling to balance their commitment to teaching with a desire to remain serious, professionally active scholars. A call to make the causes of the poor the center of our teaching and research, as well as the center of our service to the community, might easily be interpreted as an attack on our academic freedom and intellectual development, and, as such, detrimental to our educational

---

52. Jon Sobrino, S.J., "The University's Christian Inspiration." Presented June 4, 1987 at the Centenary celebration of University of Deusto, Bilbao, and published in *Estudios Centroamericanos*, no. 468, October 1987. Reprinted in *Companions of Jesus: The Jesuit Martyrs in El Salvador* (Maryknoll, N.Y.: Orbis Books), 152.

endeavors.

Our concern with the description of the Christian university offered by Sobrino is tempered by our knowledge of the environment that produced his forceful essay. We know, for instance, that Sobrino's thinking about the Christian inspiration of the university and Ignacio Ellacuria's graduation address at the University of Santa Clara entitled "Task of a Christian University"[53] were influenced by their experiences at the Catholic university in San Salvador. Both Ellacuria and Sobrino emphasized the inevitability of "persecution" by the "powerful" if a university "fights for justice" (Ellacuria) or truly follows its "Christian inspiration" (Sobrino). This prediction of hardship and persecution was tragically fulfilled in November 1989.

Because our educational methods and lifestyles have evolved in response to an environment that is quite different from theirs, we recognize that a direct application of many of their principles and models would be inappropriate. Nevertheless, a flexible interpretation or softening of their model is difficult to suggest in light of the life-defining or life-consuming commitment they demonstrated. Not surprisingly, then, we would do better to consider how the current situation at Holy Cross could be modified in response to the principles of the preferential option arguments rather than to modify the preferential option model in light of the Holy Cross experience.

In this regard, we need to consider the central place of the poor and powerless within our institutional dialogue. Our mission statement calls attention to the issue. To be a member of the Holy Cross community, we are told, is to consider "the moral character of learning and teaching," the various approaches to finding "meaning in life and history," the nature of "our obligations to one another" and "our special responsibility to the world's poor and powerless." Each of these concerns can be viewed as a reasonable progression from and an application of the one that precedes it. It is significant that an inquiry into the "moral character of teaching and learning" progresses to the final haunting question of "What is our special responsibility to the world's poor and powerless?"

Perhaps the most notable aspect of this ultimate question is not in what it asks but in what it assumes. The call is for a debate on the nature of the "special responsibility" rather than on whether we actually have this responsibility. Furthermore, that we are willing to

---

53. Ignacio Ellacuria, S.J., "The Task of a Christian University." Presented June 12, 1982 at the University of Santa Clara and published in *Companions of Jesus*, 147.

describe the responsibility as "special" implies an acknowledgement that our obligation goes beyond simply eliminating bias and prejudice from our actions. In general, we do not find the tying of this special responsibility to our mission as threatening. We know the authors of this phrase and, unlike the outspoken proponents of a preferential option, they are among us, working and teaching within our environment. They obviously do not mean to imply that we should adopt personal or institutional poverty as a part of this responsibility.

A case can be made, however, for significant overlap between the special responsibility clause of our mission statement and the principle of a preferential option. In an attempt to interpret some of the more controversial elements of the preferential option writings for a broader academic community, Stephen Pope has translated "preferential option of the poor" as "special care for the needy."[54] Pope acknowledges that it is difficult to accept that God either has or expects a preferential love for one class of citizen. It is, however, within our human experience to exhibit a "special care" or presumably, to accept, as we have done at Holy Cross, a "special responsibility." Christine Gudorf from Xavier University in Cincinnati illustrates this with the example of parental concern for a sick child.[55] Although a parent loves all children equally, it is expected that a sick child will get special care.

In another context, Pope provides an even stronger link between the phrase the College has adopted ("special responsibility") and the actions urged by the proponents of a preferential option.[56] He describes two responses of Christians to the plight of the poor. It is possible, he argues, to exercise a preferential option to the poor without a direct involvement with the poor. This "general" response includes sympathetic actions when the poor are encountered or involved in one's normal activities. On the other hand, some Christians will show a "special" response that involves activities designed to place the individual (or presumably the institution) directly in the path of the

---

54. See his article "Proper and Improper Partiality."

55. Christine E. Gudorf, "Preferential Option: Greater Challenge to the Poor" in *Victimization: Examining Christian Complicity* (Philadelphia: Trinity Press International, 1992).

56. Stephen J. Pope, "The Preferential Option for the Poor: An Ethic for Saints and Heroes?", *Irish Theological Quarterly* (in press), excerpted from Patrick H. Byrne, "*Resentiment* and the Preferential Option for the Poor," *Theological Studies* 54 (1993), 240.

poor. By acknowledging a special rather than a general responsibility to the poor and powerless in our mission statement we have, according to Pope's classifications, identified for ourselves an active and direct role in developing for the poor a preferential option.

From both our mission statement and our longstanding tradition of a concern for social justice we can safely conclude that many at Holy Cross share with Sobrino, Ellacuria and their colleagues a vision for a more just society. Further, we share their belief that a value-centered college can play a major role in bringing forth reality from the vision. However, few of us accept their model for how a university should be structured to accomplish this. Our difference of opinion on this aspect is not unexpected. In his speech at Santa Clara, Ellacuria acknowledged that such a response was likely:

> There are two aspects to a university. The first and most evident is that it has to do with culture, with knowledge, the use of the intellect. The second, not so evident, is that it must be concerned with social reality -- precisely because a university is inescapably a social force: it must transform and enlighten the society in which it lives. But how does it do that? . . . . There is no abstract and consistent answer here. *A university cannot always and in every place be the same. We should always look at our peculiar historical reality.*[57]

Following this advice, we again focus first on our current educational model. It is central to this model that faculty teach within their expertise and students have available to them courses from a wide range of disciplines. Further, we acknowledge that to remain effective, professional educators must be free to pursue scholarly activities of their own choosing. So, while some at Holy Cross may choose to focus their course content and scholarly investigations on issues that directly relate to the poor, it is unreasonable, and to our view unwise, to suggest that this be true of the entire faculty.

This appears to bring us into direct conflict with Sobrino's call for making the concerns of the poor central to all of the university's activities. Nevertheless, many in our community agree with Sobrino's related contention that an institution benefits from a common sense of purpose. A number of our successful educational experiments of recent years (for example, Interdisciplinary Studies and the First Year

---

57. "The Task of a Christian University," 149. Emphasis added.

Program) contain elements of common effort while retaining aspects of disciplinary autonomy. It is worth considering whether we can find ways to make our focus on a special responsibility to the poor more universal without encroaching on the individual and academic diversity that is so much a part of our liberal arts tradition.

A reasonable starting point is to consider what it is that we are uniquely suited to accomplish with respect to the poor. At Holy Cross, as at many relatively small liberal arts institutions, we offer all students an environment in which they can develop and enrich the life of the mind. In so doing we ensure that they have an interesting self as a lifelong companion. Further, we empower our students to overcome physical obstacles to a dignified and secure existence. Knowledge is power, and for many students it will be this power that will allow them to overcome class, race or sex-based obstacles imposed by the existing order. Finally, by promoting reasoned inquiry, we chip away at the prejudices and injustices that complicate our interpersonal actions. Each of these functions of the academy can have a positive impact on the plight of the poor and powerless. In fact, one is tempted to sidestep the entire issue by stating that our special responsibility to the poor, or the promotion of a preferential option for the poor, is best served by simply protecting the classical liberal arts environment.

It is easy to verify the profound impact our liberally educated graduates have had on society as a whole. Through many of our students, faculty have made an indirect but undeniably positive impact on the world's poor. Nevertheless, it is certainly true that the greatest benefits of a Holy Cross education accrue directly and primarily to the student. If, as Sobrino suggests, all aspects of our personal and institutional activities should have a direct impact on the poor, there is a need to ensure that the poor compose a significant fraction of our student body.

An important distinction needs to be made here. Many institutions use need-blind admission policies and nearly all offer need-based financial aid. While these are of some benefit to the poor, they do not constitute a policy of preferentially seeking out the poor. If students that are admitted for other praiseworthy reasons (e.g., academic or athletic excellence; geographic, ethnic or racial balance) happen to have need, they are given financial assistance. In general, though, students are not sought out simply because they are poor. The preferential option approach suggests that we should seek out students as a result of their poverty rather than simply accounting for the poverty of students that we seek out for other reasons.

To be sure, those born to power and privilege can benefit from what we offer. In fact, many would argue that in some respects they are the most needy. A particularly strong argument might be made that our efforts to promote social justice by sensitizing our students have the greatest impact when presented to students of privilege. Sobrino did not dismiss this as an unimportant consideration. When he viewed education in an environment where the powerful were directly killing the powerless, he acknowledged that it was appropriate to focus on education about the poor rather than direct education of the poor. At that time and in that place, the need to present the plight of the poor to the powerful was the overriding concern. Ours is a somewhat less violent setting where it may be more appropriate to balance our resources more evenly between sensitizing the powerful and educating the poor.

With respect to our goal of enriching the mental lives and empowering the physical lives of our students, we have much to offer the poor and the non-poor alike. In terms of our important role of promoting human dignity and the need to work for justice, Gudorf argues that the role of the poor in engineering these efforts is absolutely crucial and subject to greater challenges than the role of the powerful.[58] Interestingly, Sergio Canas, an institute planner at the Catholic university in San Salvador, recently noted that with the end of direct hostilities the focus of his institution has turned from working for the poor to working with the poor.[59]

Our search for a proper balance between educating students for others and educating the "others" is affected and complicated by many factors. The discussion of preference within the preferential option debate is worth considering here. Gudorf's analogy about a parent's tendency to provide preferential or special care to a sick child is very apt. The question for the parents is not who will benefit most from their limited time and resources, but who has the greatest need. Clearly, the parent loves the healthy child as well and will not withhold preventive medicine; but it is the sick child that will be given the benefits of specialized treatment and parental care. The healthy child is well situated to thrive as a result of moderate care; the sick child is afforded the special treatment without anticipation that he or she will

---

58. See Gudorf, *Victimization*, 29-53.

59. "An Activist University in an Era of Peace," *Chronicle of Higher Education* (September 15, 1993), A41.

ever be the more robust or healthy child.

The implication is that if we consider our institution to be among the country's strongest undergraduate institutions, we should be looking for students that are in greatest need of our expertise rather than looking only for those that are best prepared to respond to it. If one visits both the prestigious institutions and those institutions populated primarily by the poor and disadvantaged students, the disparity in opportunity is striking. Students with the strongest backgrounds study and relax in an inspiring setting. They can avail themselves of the most modern resources, often enjoying the luxury of low student teacher ratios while they learn from the "best and brightest" instructors. Students who have previously faced substandard educational opportunities (often in both the institutional and home environment) are typically offered the chance to redeem themselves in overcrowded, understaffed and underfunded facilities that often are characterized by substandard equipment and an uninspiring physical environment. In essence, our educational structure tends to place the healthiest students in intensive care while it offers outpatient treatment to those with critical needs.

All analogies break down at some point, and a comparison between education and health care is far from perfect. One of the differences is the major role that cooperative interactions among students has in the educational process. It is hard to overestimate the importance of peer discussions and debates in stimulating campus intellectual life. Here diversity of thought, educational background, life experiences and cultural values are crucial. Students with an unusually strong high school background have much to offer. They provide a knowledge base and procedural expertise to the group interaction. They offer more to the mix than simply the fact that they have the financial resources to make the tuition payments that fund the institution.

In the same vein, the economically and educationally disadvantaged students offer more than the opportunity for the institution to fulfill its mission. They may bring with them a particularly strong work ethic, an appreciation for the sanctity of the natural environment, a unique set of life experiences, etc. The point is that it does not make sense to advocate developing a student body drawn exclusively from either advantaged or disadvantaged students. Students who have previously benefitted from the best educational background contribute to our being a first-rate institution. They play an important role in making us the type of institution that is desirable and should be accessible to students from all backgrounds.

With the advantages of diversity come the challenges of

establishing a curriculum that is appropriate for students of dramatically different backgrounds. However, as a liberal arts institution we have a tradition of adapting our curriculum to draw from the benefits of different skills. For example, we have made the decision that there is an advantage to having students with an interest in the sciences studying alongside students with an interest in the fine arts. We advocate the value of having future accountants taking the same introductory literature courses as budding poets. In essence, we have decided that the benefits from mixing different points of view and ways of knowing are sufficient to justify our adjusting courses and curricula to accommodate diversity.

The same level of effort and creativity is called for in devising courses and curricula that accommodate widely different types of pre-college preparation. Because there are already too many demands on the time and loyalties of college faculties, this will only happen if individuals, then departments and ultimately the institution, develop a vision for both our "special responsibility to the world's poor" and the rich contribution that they can make to our diverse community. Many concerns need to be addressed to accommodate the vision. I will close this paper with two areas that are of particular concern to me.

REDESIGNING THE GATEWAY

There are a number of courses that have come to be referred to as "gateway" or "gatekeeper" courses. They serve as the prerequisite or entry way into entire fields of study. For instance, General Chemistry watches over the gate that leads into medicine, engineering, the life sciences and many other fields. Calculus guards the gate to each of these fields, as well as to economics.

These courses are of particular concern because they can serve to lock a student immediately and permanently out of a particular discipline. Many of the disciplines guarded by the gatekeepers are vertical in nature. That is, courses must be taken in a prescribed sequence. If a student cannot immediately pass through the gateway course, he or she will not be able to complete the required progression over four years. Success in these important courses is called for before students have had a chance to overcome unconventional or non-traditional preparation for college. The situation is exacerbated because elite high schools recognize these courses as crucial to the success of their students. Consequently, the courses are made the focus of intensive college preparatory curricula designed to give students who are already the best prepared a greater head start. It is in these most important courses that economically and educationally weak students are at the greatest disadvantage.

One response to this challenge is the development of teaching methodologies for the gateway courses that do not rely as heavily on the content of the high school courses. The effort and innovation invested in these courses over the last five years at Holy Cross and across the country is encouraging. In my discipline of chemistry, there is a dramatic move away from an emphasis on a uniform set of facts and concepts toward a focus on the processes of investigation. To the extent that facts and content are still emphasized there is a move to place them in a frame of reference that differs from that used in the college preparatory courses. The emphasis on cooperative learning and methods of investigation allow the group to benefit from the knowledge of the well-prepared students as one part of an overall process that encourages and rewards innovation and creativity.

The benefits are significant. Disadvantaged students experience a more level playing field. They do not compete with students who are merely fine tuning concepts they learned in high school. They experience the rewards of contributing to the group process as their creativity and familiarity with the concepts introduced earlier in the course are often more immediately relevant than the traditional background information that they are gradually acquiring. The development of these courses has served to benefit the better-prepared students as well, providing them with a course that opens new horizons rather than reviewing previous material.

A second approach being considered for accommodating poorly prepared students in gateway courses is the development of enhanced sections of introductory courses. These sections would have additional lecture or laboratory meetings each week to supplement the material that is common to the other sections of the course. This approach is consistent with our commitment to demand of all students the same intellectual rigor while acknowledging that some students have greater needs. Students can then enter the typical intermediate and advanced courses after completing the enhanced gateway course. Needless to say, there is still a great deal of work to be done in revising the gateway courses so that they can accommodate and benefit students from dramatically different high school experiences. But the effort will surely be worthwhile, not only because it is central to our liberal arts tradition, but also because it will strengthen the College's continued commitment to social justice.

RESPECTING CULTURAL DIVERSITY

An attempt at integrating the principle of a preferential option for the poor with the educational mission of Holy Cross would not be complete without reference to the importance of respecting the dignity and honoring the culture of all students within the community. This concern is highlighted in the final Puebla document of the Latin American bishops. They stated: "[Indigenous cultures] are the peoples' treasure. We commit ourselves to looking on them with sympathy and respect and to promoting them."[60] During this year of our anniversary celebration, we honor the College's rich heritage and look to this heritage as an asset as we continue with the struggles of education. The task of addressing our special responsibility to the poor and powerless will draw heavily from our individual and collective traditions within the liberal arts and our value-centered education. We will also need to acknowledge the importance of allowing our students to draw upon their personal cultural heritage and traditions as they accomplish their education. College is a time for dramatic change in most of our students. Change is, of course, exciting and exhilarating. It can also be frightening, particularly when it occurs in an unfamiliar environment. To fully explore new ideas our students need to feel the security of an anchor to the past.

It is tempting for us to evaluate a student's preconceived notions and prejudices and decide that he or she needs to start with a fresh slate. This is particularly true when we are dealing with disadvantaged students who are likely to have what the existing academic community considers as non-traditional or unsophisticated views and opinions. Like the slash and burn approach to farming, we are tempted to see it as more efficient to plant our ideas in completely cleared ground. In so doing we run the risk of shocking the system to the point that we lose entirely the opportunity to nurture fresh ideas. Certainly many students come to us with poorly developed ideas and illogical thought processes. If they did not, they would have little need for what we do. But they also bring ideas and traditions which, while perhaps unfamiliar to us, have developed within their family or local culture over many generations. It is our challenge to allow them to draw strength from these traditions while we encourage them to expand their horizons.

---

60. Paragraph 1164. See Eagleson and Scharper, *Puebla and Beyond*, 267.

Consequently, the specific meaning of the term "poor" in the Beatitudes is those actually poor and oppressed people who, having only God to depend on, do so with a messianic hope. In short, the poor of the Gospels are the materially poor who are also poor in spirit. They are . . . the actual oppressed, disadvantaged, and powerless who have the spiritual poverty of those who depend on God alone. They are the ones who grasp the reign of God and see it as vindicating the rights of the oppressed, not in granting them hegemony over their erstwhile oppressors, but in creating conditions for a truly fraternal way of life. The exaltation of the humble and the casting down of the mighty occur not in a crude reversal of the previous relationship of domination but in the emergence of solidarity. The reign of God comes in favor of all by coming in favor of the poor. . .

-- John O'Brien, *Theology and the Option for the Poor*

10.
A Preferential Option for the Poor: Social Justice and Curriculum Reform

Gary P. DeAngelis[61]

During the past five years at Holy Cross, we have been engaged in the process of defining more clearly our mission as a Catholic institution of higher learning in the 1990's. While we continue to "pursue excellence in teaching, learning and research" we also affirm our commitment to the "service of faith and the promotion of justice." If indeed we are calling our students to live a life characterized by service to others, and in fact to the most needy, then it becomes incumbent upon us as an educational institution not only to show this concern in our rhetoric and extracurricular activities but to integrate it into our curriculum.

The problem, of course, is to determine how this can be done. It is this issue that I would like to address within the context of the preferential option for the poor and what that implies for a Catholic liberal arts college. The idea of a preferential option for the poor not only helps us to focus on the issue of service to others, but it also presents us with a serious challenge regarding our educational mission. More than just service to others, it turns our attention to the most needy, both economically and politically, and the underlying reasons

---

61. Gary DeAngelis is the Associate Director of the Center for Interdisciplinary and Special Studies at Holy Cross. He also teaches Asian religions in the Religious Studies Department.

for their condition. In addition, it requires that we not only address the crises of poverty and disenfranchisement but also that we learn to look at the world and God through the eyes of the poor.

With Christ viewed as the quintessential servant, who ultimately sacrificed his own life for others, Christians are continually called to a life of sacrifice and service. Two thousand years later, as the economic gap between those who have and those who have not is as wide as ever, as political and economic disenfranchisement in the Third World threatens world stability, as the violation of basic human rights continues almost unabated in many parts of the world, the church has renewed its call for service to the disenfranchised in the form of a preferential option for the poor.

While one could argue that we all lead impoverished lives to a greater or lesser degree, either economically or spiritually, the preferential option for the poor is meant to focus our attention and concerns primarily on the economically and politically oppressed. In a very real sense it is a theological imperative which, as Steven Pope suggests, "places the misery of the poor and oppressed at the center of Christian life and thought."[62]

This imperative requires more than simply shifting the poor from the peripheral to the focal within the scope of Christian concern. It requires a new theological perspective; or, as Marcello Azevedo claims, this imperative calls for "an epistemological option, that is, a new way of seeing things, a new social perspective. One comes to see and perceive, analyze and interpret the reality in which one lives from the viewpoint of the poor."[63]

So a preferential option requires more than just social action or service; it necessitates an understanding of the perspective of the poor, to see the world and God through the eyes of the poor.

Pope asserts that the gospel calls each Christian to ask: "what am I doing in response to human suffering and misery?" He adds that the advocates of a preferential option "insist that each Christian, along with the church as a whole, be committed to changing destructive and inhumane social structures." Clearly, the structural causes of poverty and suffering need to be addressed and changed; but a preferential option necessitates a dialectic encompassing social action inspired and

---

62. Steven Pope, "Necessary Option," *Boston College Magazine* (Spring 1993), 34.

63. Marcello Azevedo, S.J. "Semantics of the Option for the Poor," *Promotio Justitiae* 52 (August 1993), 4.

informed by this "new way of seeing things." So in light of our mission and the "preferential option" our task becomes twofold: on the one hand, we need to instruct students regarding issues of social justice and social responsibility and, on the other hand, we need somehow to enable them to enter the world of the other and see the world through the eyes of the poor.

One question for us, if we are to take the College's mission statement seriously, has to be: How do we educate our students for life and specifically a life in service to others? The carrying out of the mission can manifest itself in many ways; but above all the mission must be an integral part of the curriculum, which lies at the heart of the institution. To be sure, we are not a seminary. We are a liberal arts college providing a solid program of liberal learning in the arts, humanities and sciences and preparing our students for fulfilling and productive lives and careers in many professions -- careers in which they will have a significant impact on local, national and foreign policy and the quality of life in their own communities and beyond.

While we may have much in common with institutions such as Williams, Bowdoin, Amherst and Colgate, we are also different. We are a Jesuit institution, dedicated to the intellectual life and committed to the service of faith and the promotion of justice. It is this difference that we need to nurture, develop and celebrate. This difference is clearly manifested in our mission statement and I would suggest that we have a profound moral obligation not only to affirm beliefs and values that address a preferential option for the poor, but also somehow to teach how these beliefs and values can become manifest in action, how they can become integrated into our professional and personal lives and how they can, in effect, integrate our professional and personal lives in direct service to the poor.

Contrary to the misplaced fears of some, the mission statement does not imply or necessitate some kind of a "Catholic" slant on every course or discipline. Yet what I think it does call for is that, in some way, the College's curriculum reflect our concern and commitment to Christian values. That does not mean merely pointing to a religious studies department as symbolizing our Catholicity, but it has something to do with our whole educational philosophy.

Of course, we are a pre-professional school and it would be disingenuous to deny this. Yet more importantly, we are committed to liberal learning, and to liberal learning with a decidedly humanistic base, because of our Catholic orientation. However, it is our responsibility as a Jesuit College not just to pay lip service to these values, but to nurture them in numerous ways and make it clear that they can and should be integrated into what we do here. I see integration as the key, particularly in reference to the curriculum. As David O'Brien pointed out, we need to think through the relationship between research, learning and social responsibility.

We are dealing with a very basic issue here of what it means to be truly human in a Christian context. The salient issue is not whether we should volunteer at a soup kitchen or donate to charities, but rather how we should live our lives. If we affirm that we are to live as men and women for others, then, if we are truly educating our students for life, we must make it clear how this can be done, how one integrates moral values and concerns with one's life's work. It is both too easy and too irresponsible to pass this task on to a religious studies department.

Certainly, departments of theology and religious studies can play an important role in this endeavor. But moral concerns and ethical issues must be taken seriously by all departments if we are to make it clear to our students that these issues are not abstract and reserved solely for their spiritual and personal lives, but that they will bear upon their professional lives as well. The unique role of a Jesuit institution should be to show students how this can be done. We cannot assume that training students in political science and economics and having them take courses in theology and philosophy will somehow, magically, enable them to see the connection. In some ways what we end up doing is perpetuating the separation, the compartmentalization that has led to the general malaise affecting our political and economic institutions. People tend, all too often, to operate with a kind of moral schizophrenia, a split between the professional amoral self and the spiritual moral self which remains secluded in one's private life.

Once again, I would suggest that in order for students to make a serious and effective commitment to issues of social injustice and oppression they need to know not only the structural causes of poverty, but they also need to understand what the world looks like through the eyes of the impoverished and oppressed. It is this new vision combined with understanding and faith that will enable our students to transform our institutions in service of a more just society.

Addressing the demands of our mission statement and the option for the poor does not necessitate a radical overhauling of the curriculum. I think that it is possible through curriculum innovations not only to respond to these concerns and issues but also to make it clear that concern for these issues is inherently a part of the uniqueness of this institution. While some of these innovations could be developed by the Center for Interdisciplinary and Special Studies, it is essential, for the success of this initiative, that a number of departments make a serious commitment to this undertaking.

I think that there are three basic areas of development within the curriculum which could clearly address our commitment to these issues. The first is the area of general course offerings. What is needed in this area is the development of additional courses in sociology, psychology, political science, etc., dealing specifically with issues of poverty and disenfranchisement, focussing on the perspective of the poor as well as the structural causes and effects of poverty.

The second area of curriculum development, which is essential, if we are to deal seriously with the issue of comprehending the experience of the poor, is an increased emphasis on experiential learning. This initiative could be undertaken at two levels. The first level would be within the framework of our Semester Away Program. Building on our student volunteer programs in Appalachia and Mexico, we could develop internship programs which combine academic and experiential components in both rural and urban poverty areas. This program could focus on a number of diverse areas, e.g., economic development, community organizing, public health, etc. A second level would be a program dealing with some of these same issues at the local scene. This component is already in place in the form of our Academic Internship Program. This program provides students with the opportunity to undertake an internship in the local community combined with a seminar related to their internship experience. One seminar that specifically addresses the issues of poverty is entitled "Social Justice." While students participate in internships in various social service agencies throughout the City and develop a sense of the experience of the impoverished, they are also learning how to relate this experience both to their personal lives and to the larger context of community, culture and the earth as a whole. Whether the focus be local or global, this course, through direct experience and critical analysis of that experience, brings the student to an ever increasing recognition of the inherent interconnectedness and interdependence among all who live on this increasingly fragile planet and one's personal responsibility for social justice.

Another seminar, "Ethical Issues in Professional Life," concentrates more on the structural causes of poverty, injustice and disenfranchisement by exposing students to the professional scene -- institutional life in law, medicine, business, and journalism, for instance -- while critically examining ethical and moral issues associated with these professions. In both courses students explore issues of social responsibility and how one moves from an intellectual analysis of ethical issues to a life that is honorable and decent. Whether the experiential component is carried out locally or far removed from campus, it is a critical aspect in sensitizing our students to the perspective of the poor and the ability to understand not just the consequences of poverty but its essence.

A third curriculum innovation which could certainly focus our mission goals and our concerns for a preferential option for the poor would be the development of a program in ethics across the curriculum. Such a program, staffed by the philosophy and religious studies departments, could provide recommendations and guidance to faculty in different departments on how to integrate ethical concerns and issues into their courses.

There are certainly other possibilities for curriculum development worth considering and, as a college, this is where our concern for the poor should be focused. We may espouse particular beliefs and values, we may encourage our students to engage in service to others, we may provide institutional support to charities; but as an educational institution the curriculum must clearly, in an on-going way, define and promote our values and mission. In the end, what I am calling for is a curriculum that will allow our students to re-imagine a society that is more just at many different levels. Without that sense of vision nothing will change significantly.

What I am advocating is the development, within the curriculum, of interdisciplinary and experiential learning courses that will specifically address these concerns and further characterize Holy Cross as an institution that not only has a strong commitment to the value of liberal learning but is equally concerned that learning be focussed, in part, on issues of social justice. The hope, ultimately, for the poor (and surely for all of us, because their poverty and lack of empowerment diminishes us all) is for the transformation of society into one that seriously commits itself to the well-being of all of its members.

If we take our mission seriously and if we truly believe that education should have a civilizing influence, i.e., produce compassionate persons, then it is incumbent upon us to educate our students not only to be accomplished physicians, lawyers, leaders and business people, but equally to be caring, sensitive, humane leaders. The task is not only to serve the poor and oppressed through charity and volunteer work. Even more importantly the task is to develop enlightened, compassionate individuals who will provide the leadership that will transform the society and the system which perpetuate the inequities among us. We must enable our students to see that there is social injustice, that if we are not part of the solution, then we have become part of the problem. One's life work can and must address the challenge of justice in some way.

Liberation theology, in its call for a preferential option for the poor, may actually be summoning us to a much more radical transformation than what I am advocating. Perhaps it is calling for a serious re-examination of what we even mean by education and questioning whether, in fact, we are in reality contributing to the perpetuation of a system that promotes human suffering and misery. I am not sure.

I am concerned with what we can do right now -- with what this institution, in light of its mission, can do realistically to educate its students to transform destructive and inhumane social structures. We can focus our concern on the causes of human suffering and misery as an integral part of our mission and show how each person's place in society offers possibilities for contributing to the common good. In exercising a preferential option for the poor we will not only be carrying out a mission of social responsibility, but in looking at the world and God through the eyes of the poor and disenfranchised we will also become further humanized in ways perhaps undreamed of.

Finding one's voice, witnessing to experience, communicating with fellow human beings is an integral part of literature as well as religion. Without words, oral or written, the divine Word would not come alive. It is therefore an abridgement of human rights as well as a perversion of religion when masses of women for ages have been kept silent, uneducated, and relegated to "natural," brainless, wordless tasks of their bodies. Up to this day, millions of them are not even respected in their bodies. "Violence against women comprises at present the greatest violation of human rights throughout the earth."

The words of women will not let injustice be buried forever. There will always be "a woman singing in the midst of chaos."

-- Kristin Herzog, *Finding Their Voice:*
    Peruvian Women's Testimonies of War

11.
Women and the Option for the Poor

Mary Ann Hinsdale, I.H.M.[64]

My topic concerns the option for the poor and women. David Hummon spoke about the option for the poor and children. He presented us with empirical evidence which helped to unpack an important aspect of understanding what is meant by the phrase "preferential option for the poor." His statistics showed us that more children are counted among the poor in the recent past than any other group, and that children in the United States are more likely to be born poor than children from other industrialized countries. The reasons for this are complex and have to do, he explains, with class structure, the erosion of government support for the poor, the changing family structure and discrimination based on race and gender.

I am a theologian, not a sociologist, and although I am also in the field of women's studies, an interdisciplinary field which draws upon the methodologies of the social sciences, my approach will be a little different. I am not going to quote the parallel statistics which could be presented to convince us that when we speak of the poor, we speak

64. Mary Ann Hinsdale, I.H.M., is an Associate Professor of Theology at Holy Cross. She received her Ph.D. from the University of St. Michael's College in 1984. Her areas of teaching and research include ecclesiology, Christian anthropology, hermeneutics and feminist theory. Her publications include *Faith That Transforms* (Paulist Press, 1987), *"It Comes From the People": Community Development and Local Theology* (Temple University Press [in press]), and *Hans Kung's Use of Scripture* (Peter Lang [also in press]), as well as many articles in theological journals.

primarily of women. The majority of single parents are women, and where one finds children, particularly small children in a situation of dependence, one usually finds their mothers or another female caretaker with them in the same situation of economic poverty. Among the elderly poor, too, we find that the majority are women.[65]

HISTORY OF THE CONCEPT

An historical investigation of the notion of the "option for the poor" (not merely the phrase itself) shows that far from being an invention of Latin American liberation theology, this notion "has a long history which encompasses many of the earliest Christian writers, much of medieval tradition and even such revered saints of the Protestant tradition as John Wesley."[66] The Bible itself, of course, long before Christianity came upon the scene, demonstrates the preferential option for the poor in God's liberation of the people of Israel from their slavery in Egypt under Pharaoh:

> Then the Lord said, "I have observed the misery of my people who are in Egypt; I have heard their cry on account of their taskmasters. Indeed, I know their sufferings, and I have come down to deliver them from the Egyptians, and to bring them to a good and broad land, a land flowing with milk and honey." (Exodus 3:7-8)

This paradigm was taken up by Christianity in its interpretation of Jesus as a new Moses who would be the prophetic herald of a movement into a new land, a promised land, which was not otherworldly, but began concretely in the construction of an ethic and a society here and now which embodied the values of justice, peace, economic equity, etc. Two passages from the New Testament which embody both the vision of this liberating experience and its radicality, in terms of an implication for Christian discipleship, are the Magnificat

---

65. Documentation for my assertion that most of the world's poor are women, as well as the children dependent upon them, can be found in Joni Seager and Ann Olson, *Women in the World: An International Atlas* (New York: Simon & Schuster, 1986).

66. Justo Gonzalez, "The Option for the Poor in Latin American Liberation Theology" in *Poverty and Ecclesiology: Nineteenth-Century Evangelicals in the Light of Liberation Theology* (Collegeville: Liturgical Press, 1992), 9. I rely on Gonzalez's analysis for much of what follows in this essay.

of Mary and Jesus' Sermon on the Mount. The scholarly discussion about the historicity of these words is not at issue. What is at issue is that they have been preserved by the Christian community as paradigmatic of the same conviction which underlies the experience of Exodus, namely, that God stands with the poor, the enslaved, the marginalized. These New Testament texts are radical sayings and they make us uncomfortable. But this is what I believe the "preferential option for the poor" has as its heart.

Luke 1:46-55 records Mary's response to the angel who announces the birth of this "new Moses." Both Luke (in 6:20-26) and Matthew (in 5:1-12) collect a series of "blessings" and compile them into a speech put on the lips of Jesus. Who will receive the blessings of the reign of God? The person hungering and thirsting for justice, those who mourn, the peacemakers, the merciful, the humble, the pure of heart, the meek, and those who suffer persecution and false accusation. These are the "preferred."

The Latin American bishops at their conference in Medellin (1968) went further than the Second Vatican Council in their understanding of "the poor." Though Vatican II was quite strong in its concern for the poor (it condemned both laissez-faire capitalism and state socialism as impeding the necessary freedom of choice for diminishing social and economic inequality), it was also condescending. Those who wished Vatican II to take a prophetic stance in favor of the poor and against the root causes of poverty were disappointed in such passages as: "the Church encompasses with love all who are afflicted with human suffering and in the poor and afflicted sees the image of its poor and suffering Founder. It does all it can to relieve their need and in them it strives to serve Christ."[67]

It was the Pastoral Constitution on the Church in the Modern World which addressed such issues as the limitation of the right to private property and brought into question the systems which make people and nations poor. For example, the decree stated:

> By its very nature, private property has a social quality deriving from the law of the communal purpose of earthly goods. If this social quality is overlooked, property often becomes an occasion of greed and of serious disturbances. Thus, to those who attack the concept of private property, a pretext is given for calling the right

67. Dogmatic Constitution on the Church, #8. See *The Sixteen Documents of Vatican II* (Boston: St. Paul Editions), 116.

itself into question.

In many underdeveloped areas there are large or even gigantic rural estates which are only moderately cultivated or lie completely idle for the sake of profit. At the same time the majority of the people are either without land or have only very small holdings, and there is evident and urgent need to increase land productivity.

It is not rare for those who are hired to work for the landowners, or who till a part of the land as tenants, to receive a wage or income unworthy of human beings, to lack decent housing, or to be exploited by middle-men. Deprived of all security, they live under such personal servitude that almost every opportunity for acting on their own initiative and responsibility is denied to them, and all advancement in human culture and all sharing in social and political life is ruled out.[68]

Unfortunately, as can now be seen in retrospect, this document did not promote the cause of the poor themselves as agents of change, but treated them as *objects* "for which and through which the church was to show its concern for justice. The poor were seen as receiving the *ministries* of the church, and even as profiting from its advocacy, but not as *agents* in the cause of justice or in the ministries of the church."[69]

This is where I see the connection between the option for the poor and women. Feminist analysis sees that at the root of the subjugation and domination of women, indeed of every class of people who are discriminated against, is the objectification of this group. They are treated as "objects" rather than as "subjects" of their own destiny. There is a long list of authors who could be cited to substantiate this analysis. The philosopher Simone de Beauvoir, author of *The Second Sex*, is perhaps one of the better known. So too the feminist ethicist Mary Daly who parodied de Beauvoir in her book *The Church and the Second Sex*.

In regard to the option for the poor, the analysis which was made

68. The Pastoral Constitution on the Church in the Modern World, #71, quoted from Joseph Gremillion, *The Gospel of Peace and Justice: Catholic Social Teaching since Pope John* (Maryknoll, N.Y.: Orbis Books, 1976), 307.

69. Gonzalez, 17.

of the situation of the poor in Latin America by the Catholic bishops at Medellin is much more radical than that of Vatican II. Indeed, these documents are much more clear about stressing the agency of the poor themselves and the conception of poverty as "primarily the result of unjust structures and economic systems."[70] Medellin makes an important step in its conceptualization of the idea of "the preferential option of the poor," which is extremely relevant to the situation of women in patriarchal society. Medellin does not see the poor as the object of charity or of concern on the part of the church. It espouses a view of empowerment which realizes that "if a more just economic order is to emerge, this will happen only if means are found to counteract the influence of those who hold the power to their own advantage." The bishops proposed a plan to develop the political consciousness of the people using small communities which sought to establish a balance with the groups in power. The small Christian communities, known as "base communities," are groups in which the poor are able to become subjects, rather than objects, of their own history.[71] This is very similar to the formation among women and other marginalized groups of "consciousness-raising" or "strategy groups."

Medellin, rather than advocating on behalf of the poor, proposed a strategy which places the poor at the very center of political, economic and ecclesiastical action. Although these communities already existed before their meeting in 1968, the bishops recognized their potential power and decided to encourage their formation for precisely that reason. By the time of their Puebla meeting in 1979, this approach became both widespread and controversial. The bishops had not counted on the possibility that some of the poor's insights about structural power and injustice would be applied to the institution of the church itself. (I find this same parallel, by the way, in the encouraging words of John XXIII's 1963 encyclical *Pacem in Terris* [Peace on Earth], Vatican II's *Gaudium et Spes*, and the document *Justice in the World* from the 1971 Synod of Bishops. These writings advocated the position of women and encouraged their participation in social process, but then drew the line when women and laity expected the church to take its own words seriously).

If one is to understand the preferential option for the poor as also

---

70. Gonzalez, 18.

71. Gonzalez, 19.

symbolizing a preferential option for women (and I might add, for the earth as well), then it is clear that to opt for the poor does not simply mean to be concerned for them, to offer them help, or to seek better economic conditions for them. Nor does it mean simply to become poor, or to spend time among the poor. All of these things may be good and even necessary; but the preferential option for the poor is more than that:

> To opt for the poor means to opt for a struggle with the poor and on their behalf. Even those who are poor, in the sense of having no possessions, must make an option for the poor, in the sense of deciding to join the poor in their struggle for justice.[72]

Along with Justo Gonzalez, I understand this primarily as a call to conversion. It is the call to choose, the call to follow, which is put forth in the gospel stories depicting the call of the first disciples. As middle-class and upperclass Christians, it is important for us not to fall into the trap of paternalism/maternalism and call that an option for the poor. What is required is not a decision to help the poor, but "to understand the pain of the poor and the reasons that make them poor."[73] Then one must cast one's lot with the poor, not helping through charity, but helping to struggle for a different social order. This theme is strikingly clear in the final document from the Latin American bishops who met in Puebla in 1979.[74]

According to Gonzalez, this conversion demands more. First, it involves partisan action, taking sides on behalf of the poor and their struggle, or what might be termed a "political conversion." Secondly, it demands a different way of conceiving knowledge, a new way of seeing, or what might be termed an "epistemological conversion." Thirdly, it demands being with the poor, living in solidarity with them in order to learn from their experience.

The base Christian communities are a place where the "church *of*

72. Gonzalez, 21. See also the essays in Paul Plenge Parker, ed., *Standing with the Poor: Theological Reflections on Economic Reality* (Cleveland: The Pilgrim Press, 1992).

73. Gonzalez, 21.

74. See John Eagleson and Philip Scharper, eds., *Puebla and Beyond* (Maryknoll, N.Y.: Orbis Books, 1979).

the poor" has become a reality. Through reading the Bible for themselves, in light of their own experience, the poor have come up with surprising and fresh interpretations. If it is true that Jesus came to preach "good news to the poor," why have we not listened to their interpretation of his gospel? Again, my experience in women's groups -- both poor and non-poor -- shows me that these same conversions are applicable in the attaining of feminist insight.

Since 1968 I have been involved in a participatory research project which concerns the survival of a small, rural community in southern Appalachia.[75] Ivanhoe, Virginia, a little town "on the rough side of the mountain," lost its remaining industry in 1981. Determined not to let their community die, the women of Ivanhoe began a revitalization movement which also contributed to the transformation of their consciousness of themselves as women. Although not all women in Ivanhoe would be comfortable with the label "feminist," the word "conversion" is a word with which they are quite comfortable. Their stories, which are chronicled in Ivanhoe's community-produced history book, tell of how the entire community became "converted" to a new way of seeing.[76] Reflecting in light of the Gospel on the injustice and betrayal of the mining company which abandoned them, they began to realize that their oppression was not "the will of God," nor had they done anything "bad" which would justify the plant closings. They began to educate themselves about the economic causes for Ivanhoe's decline and at the same time began to discover their own inherent dignity as knowing "subjects" who could not only understand their predicament, but who could seek to change it. For the women, this education/reflection process gave birth not only to a new vision of community, in which each person "had a say and a share," but also to new realizations concerning themselves as women and shapers of the community's destiny.

According to characteristics listed by Elizabeth Johnson, I believe that the reflections which emerged from the Ivanhoe women's Bible

---

75. The Ivanhoe story is documented in Mary Ann Hinsdale, Helen M. Lewis and Maxine Walter, *"It Comes from the People": Community Development and Local Theology* (Philadelphia: Temple University Press, forthcoming).

76. Helen M. Lewis and Suzanna O'Donnell, eds., *Remembering Our Past, Building Our Future* (Ivanhoe, VA: Ivanhoe Civic League, 1990). Many of these stories, as well as the women's Bible reflections, are also included in *"It Comes From the People"*, cited above.

discussions mirror Gonzalez' three-fold conversion process. Moreover, they can also be considered "feminist theology." For Johnson, feminist theology

> arises out of the recognition of the suffering of a particular oppressed group, in this case women. Consciousness of the ways women are perpetually relegated to second-class citizenship in society and church, in contrast to women's essential human dignity, gives rise to outrage: this should not be; this is against the will of God. Reflection arises in groups actively engaged in praxis, or prayerful resistance to patriarchal oppression. Sedimented in structures, the social nature of the sin of sexism is laid bare by feminist social analysis. The goal of this form of theologizing is not only to understand the meaning of the faith tradition, but also to change it insofar as it has not meant good news for human beings who are women. Finally, the vision which guides feminist theology is that of a new human community based on the values of mutuality and reciprocity. . . [T]he dream of a new heaven and a new earth takes hold here, with no one group dominating and no one group being subordinated, but each person in his or her own right participating according to their gifts, without preconceived stereotyping, in genuine mutuality.[77]

The conversion to the experience of women as a legitimate and valuable way of knowing and to their participation as full and complete human persons in shaping that which affects human destiny is likewise demanded from all who would accept the call of an option for the poor.

---

77. Elizabeth A. Johnson, *Consider Jesus: Waves of Renewal in Christology* (New York: Crossroad Publishing Co., 1993), 98-99.

12.
Afterword: Where Do We Go from Here?

William Reiser, S.J.[78]

Prior to the formal presentation of the symposium papers, students in the College's Honors Program were given the opportunity to read and react to them. Many of their comments are both insightful and thought-provoking. One student wrote:

> As for a Christian university, I think it should, as Christian, decide on a set of values that it will uphold both within its institution and in response to the world around it. It should not compromise its stance in order to ensure monetary or political assistance. . . I think a Christian university should provide instruction in theology because a main purpose of a university is to educate; but also it should promote interaction within the [local] community since the university is part of the community and since some of the best education comes through experience.

And another student said:

> I opted for a Jesuit education because its focus is to teach each student to become someone, a complete person, as opposed to

---

78. William Reiser, S.J. teaches courses in systematic theology and spirituality. Most recently he has written *Talking About Jesus Today* (1993) and *Looking for a God to Pray to* (1994), both from Paulist Press.

merely training a person to do a job. Reaching out to others is
essential to becoming a complete person because no man or woman
stands alone. We are all members of a greater community. We all
live in this world together.

Responding to Professor Ditzler's paper, one student commented:

> Simply promoting reasoned inquiry does not necessarily break any
> barriers. I have seen enough times the students who use their "new
> power" to argue only more cunningly within the same prejudices
> they have always had.

The students often found themselves challenged by what the
writers were saying and unable to resolve the tensions which an option
for the poor sets in motion. One spoke candidly:

> I do SPUD [Student Program for Urban Development] storytelling
> at a Worcester elementary school for an hour a week, and though I
> absolutely love it, I could never say that I'm seeing through the eyes
> of the poor. I'm not living with them and fully understanding them,
> because after that hour, I go back to my secluded Holy Cross
> campus where everyone is anything but poor.

The problem of developing a solidarity with the poor is often like
trying to squeeze through the eye of a needle. Some wondered whether
their salvation was being jeopardized simply because of the fact that
they came from such advantaged backgrounds:

> If the Church is primarily for the poor, how can the Church be
> universal? How can the Church be a communion in the unity of
> Christ if the wealthy are excluded from its mission? . . . Because of
> my background, I must believe that the Church is not just for the
> poor -- it is for the spiritually poor who need God to develop their
> faith. Remember Jesus' words from the Beatitudes: "Happy are the
> poor in spirit, for theirs is the kingdom of God."

And another felt the same way:

> Does the expression, "The first shall be last and the last shall be
> first," really mean that the rich will not be saved because they are
> not disadvantaged on earth? There are many ways to be
> disadvantaged. Material poverty is not the only form of poverty and

it would be wrong to assume that the rich have easy lives just because they have money.

One of the spiritual tensions produced by talk about the option for the poor takes the form of feeling guilty:

> But liberation theology is meant to free the economic poor from oppression. It is not to be imposed on middle class students so that they feel less loved by God, guilty for what they have, or less able to fulfill their role as Christian adults.

While the student reactions included many comments related specifically to issues which were addressed in the individual papers, the more telling points had to do with the concept of the option for the poor itself and what making such an option might imply for their future. Most of them were ready to buy into the concept, but they were looking for some practical suggestions about implementing the option. Responding to Carolyn Howe's paper, one student wondered whether she gave enough credit to the idea of private charity and individual reform: "It may not be the answer to the [structural] poverty question, but it is a sincere attempt on behalf of many in society." And responding to Mauri Ditzler's paper, the same student continued:

> The one weakness I see in his essay is that he could have stated some examples of the positive impact the faculty, through the students, have had on the world's poor.

Students reacted very favorably to Peter Perkins' remarks precisely because they could relate to his searching for the proper Christian way to live in an affluent society. One said:

> The author allows the reader to struggle with him through a very difficult, real problem. This interactive journey makes for active, rather than passive, reading. While he may not have arrived at any answers, [Professor Perkins] has succeeded by asking important poverty-related questions of himself and others.

Many faculty, needless to say, have struggled the same way as the students, although we approach the "practical" implications of the option for the poor from a teacher's angle. What does the option for the poor mean? What bearing should it have on our personal lives? What impact ought it to have on our professional lives as teachers and researchers? What might the option for the poor mean for us institutionally as a community of educators? Language about the option for the poor makes us uneasy, too, and in the background of our minds is our remembrance of the Catholic University in El Salvador and the commitment to truth which brought six educators to their death.

For us, thinking and wrestling with the option for the poor has to be an integral part of the educational enterprise, no matter what our academic specialization is. Many of us are persuaded that learning, teaching and research which prescind from the fundamental human realities of our time drives a wedge into knowledge itself. An ancient insight into human understanding views knowledge as participation: the mind knows by participating in the being of something else. Numerous contemporary writers have suggested that understanding is woefully incomplete when the mind seeks to dominate and control rather than experience itself as continuous with the world -- both the world of nature and the world of persons. How then could one ever think about or study the causes of poverty without ever participating in the reality of those human beings who are poor? Misery and oppression caused by injustice and inequality are not abstractions; they are concretely found in men and women. For this reason an option for the poor includes an epistemological option, that is, stepping into the social reality of the poor. Marcelo Azevedo explains:

> The *social place* of the poor is not then a social category, a position in the scale of goods or power in a society (rich or educated, professionals or manual workers). It is an *epistemological* category, a way of seeing and knowing. Everyone can possess it and those who do so best are those who discover in the poor the Gospel root of their poverty and, for this very reason, poverty's meaning and scope as well as its necessary transformation.[79]

Perhaps only the contemplative person ever truly understands anything. Immersion or insertion into the world of the poor -- something called for by faculty and students alike -- leads to understanding and solidarity only when we are prepared to let go of ourselves -- our anxieties, our insecurities, our preconceived ideas -- and listen compassionately to the lives of others.

Christian faith will never divorce the mystery of God from the human story. This is not because God is simply a projection on the part

---

79. Marcelo Azevedo, S.J., "Semantics of the Option for the Poor," *LADOC* 24:5 (May/June, 1994), 21-22.

of human consciousness, or because theology is ultimately anthropology, as some thinkers have argued. The inseparability of God from our story arises because our story is a story of God: a God who fashioned the world out of love and whose love chose to side with those on the bottom. Indeed, all of us are sinners, and all of us stand in need of divine mercy. Yet that mercy appears to have determined that the salvation of the rich and powerful would depend upon their making friends with the poor and oppressed.

The symposium provided an opportunity to explore the meaning of the option for the poor in a truly collaborative way. Although the phrase originates in a religious framework, one cannot speak about poverty without looking at its real-life context. Human beings suffer from poverty, and concretely that reality requires our attending to the political and social, as well as the economic dimensions of their lives. As a result, discussion of the option for the poor involves not only theologians, but also economists and social scientists.

Furthermore, since the option for the poor affects institutions as well as individuals, thinking about its implications for the curriculum within our particular educational institution becomes unavoidable. And if we are on the right track in saying that there is a knowing which one can only achieve through doing, then it also becomes necessary to consider those extra-curricular possibilities which might put us in direct contact with the experience of socially and economically marginalized people.

Even academic disciplines whose concerns might seem far removed from the world of the poor cannot escape being confronted by the harsh realities of our time. The question, "But whose interests are being served by what I teach or by what I study?", is an important one for us to ask ourselves. To be sure, the College has adopted a mission statement, and part of our motivation in planning the symposium and writing our papers was to keep our corporate moral spotlight on the challenges and responsibilities which that statement sets before us.

Yet we also realized that the educational enterprise itself is not immune from ideological interests. The fact is that all of our people do not enjoy equal access to educational opportunities and the empowerment which those opportunities can create. Education empowers some of us, not all; and the danger exists that those who have been empowered might not be willing to share that power, especially if that sharing will affect the way of life to which we have grown accustomed. The question about whose interests are being served thus remains a critical one in our personal and corporate examination of conscience. Even as biologists, chemists and mathematicians we have had to take a hard look at what we do and why, ultimately, we do it.

Early in our conversations we discovered that this profound sensibility with respect to the poor was something we shared, even when we did not share the same faith perspective. The reasons for this convergence are perhaps somewhat mysterious, yet oddly enough the option for the poor was not something which any of us objected to as unfounded or irrational. In fact, the option for the poor seemed to correspond to an intuition we shared about the connectedness of human beings and the profound solidarity which is ours simply because we are here, on this planet, for ever so brief a moment. There is a beatitude to be discovered in the effort of making that option.

But the reason, ultimately, for making the option for the poor is not the expectation of personal gratification in the form of some inner consolation -- feeling good -- over having done something worthwhile with one's life; nor is it simply the desire to experience a comforting oneness with other men and women in some sort of mystical communion. Certainly, the reason is not the need to do something about one's feelings of guilt over having been born into privilege and security, either. The reason, finally, why one makes the option for the poor is love. And maybe the one thing which each of us comprehended was that human beings have been made for nothing, if not for love. For a Christian, of course, this is the heart of the matter. The author of the First Letter of John wrote:

> Beloved, let us love one another, because love is from God; everyone who loves is born of God and knows God. Whoever does not love does not know God, for God is love. (1 Jn 4:7-8)

A Select Bibliography

Marcelo Azevedo, S.J., "Semantics of the Option for the Poor," *LADOC* (Latin American Documentation) 24:5 (May/June 1994), 20-24. This reflection also appeared in *Promotio Justitiae* 52 (August 1993).

Dean Brackley, S.J., "The Christian University and Liberation," *Discovery: Jesuit International Ministries* 2 (December 1992).

Patrick H. Byrne, "*Ressentiment* and the Preferential Option for the Poor," *Theological Studies* 54:2 (1993), 213-241.

Ignacio Ellacuria, S.J., "The Task of a Christian University," *Companions of Jesus*, Jon Sobrino, Ignacio Ellacuria, et. al. (Maryknoll, N.Y.: Orbis Books, 1990), 147-151.

Christine E. Gudorf, "Preferential Option: Greater Challenge to the Poor," *Victimization: Examining Christian Complicity* (Philadelphia: Trinity Press International, 1992), 28-53.

Gustavo Gutierrez, *The God of Life*, trans. Matthew O'Connell (Maryknoll, N.Y.: Orbis Books, 1992). See also his essay, "Option for the Poor," in *Mysterium Liberationis: Fundamental Concepts of Liberation Theology*, ed. Ignacio Ellacuria and Jon Sobrino (Maryknoll, N.Y.: Orbis Books, 1993), 235-250.

John Hassett and Hugh Lacey, eds., *Towards a Society That Serves Its People: The Intellectual Contribution of El Salvador's Murdered Jesuits* (Washington, D.C.: Georgetown University Press, 1993).

Seamus Murphy, S.J., "The Many Ways of Justice," *Studies in the Spirituality of Jesuits* 26:2 (March 1994).

John O'Brien, *Theology and the Option for the Poor* (Collegeville, MN: Liturgical Press, 1992).

Steven Pope, "Proper and Improper Partiality and the Preferential Option for the Poor," *Theological Studies* 54:2 (1993), 242-271.

Paul G. Shervish, ed., *Wealth in Western Thought: The Case for and against Riches* (Westport, Conn.: Praeger, 1994). Papers from an interdisciplinary seminar held at Boston College 1989 and 1990.

Jon Sobrino, S.J., "The University's Christian Inspiration," *Companions of Jesus*, Jon Sobrino, Ignacio Ellacuria, et. al. (Maryknoll, N.Y.: Orbis Books, 1990), 152-173.